W9-BKE-017

entrées

a dierbergs school of cooking publication

Acknowledgements

Director of Marketing and Advertising
John Muckerman

Editor
Barb Ridenhour

Cookbook Project Manager
Janice Martin

Copywriters
Gena Bast, Therese Lewis

Art Director/Designer
Mike Parker

Dierbergs School of Cooking Managers
Loretta Evans, Jennifer Kassel, Nancy Lorenz, Pam Pahl

Photography
Michelle Havens, Group 360 Communications
Steve Adams, Steve Adams Studio (pages 4, 93, 94)

Food Stylist
Linda Behrends, Behrends and Associates

Food Styling Assistants
Cathy Chipley, Therese Lewis, Janice Martin

Prop Stylist, Dierbergs Test Kitchen Manager
Karen Hurych

Nutrition Analysis
Trish Farano, D.T.R., Dierbergs Markets
Sherri Hoyt, R.D., Missouri Baptist Medical Center

Proofreading/Recipe Editing
Jennifer Brock, Patty Tomaselli

Contributors
Mary Billings, Sally Bruns, Denise Hall, Carolyn Pokorny,
Jeannie Rader, Carol Ziemann

Entrées
A Dierbergs School of Cooking Publication

Copyright 2006
Dierbergs Markets, Inc.
16690 Swingley Ridge Road
Chesterfield, Missouri 63017

This cookbook is a collection of recipes, which has been developed and tested by Dierbergs Home Economists.

All rights reserved. No part of this publication may be reproduced in any form or by any means, electronic or mechanical, including photocopy and information storage and retrieval systems, without permission in writing from the publisher.

ISBN: 978-0-9749955-2-6

First Printing 2006

Cover photograph:
Grilled Herb-Rubbed Chops
Recipe on page 50

TABLE OF
contents

From left to right: Greg and Susan Dierberg, Brian Dierberg, Sharon and Bob Dierberg, Laura and Dr. Jeff Padousis.

With special gratitude to the Dierberg family, for its enduring commitment to food and food education. The Dierberg family traces its grocery roots to a small country store that began serving the St. Louis community in 1854. Today's third and fourth generations have grown the business to a chain of supermarkets known for outstanding food solutions, superb service and being a pillar of the St. Louis community.

Introduction

For more information on Dierbergs School of Cooking, visit **www.dierbergs.com** or call 636-812-1336 in Missouri or 618-622-5353 in Illinois.

Nestled in the front of five Dierbergs stores are cooking schools – on first impression, they may seem unassuming – yet their presence in a supermarket is keenly purposeful. More than just a kitchen, Dierbergs cooking schools are an important link between the food and the customer.

Walk by while a class is in session or a recipe is in creation and you'll feel the excitement and force of a wondrous world of food. Step through the doors where some of the area's most respected chefs, restaurateurs, instructors and food professionals have inspired countless in the art of cooking.

As an innovator in the supermarket industry, it's no surprise that Bob Dierberg would wisely plan for cooking schools in his stores. It just makes perfect sense to offer customers a helpful resource for food education. In 1978, he pioneered the first cooking school in an American supermarket. Today, the schools and those who teach there are highly respected in the culinary world. And the recipes generated from Dierbergs School of Cooking are not only sought after but become mainstays in the collections of those who prepare them.

For more than 25 years, countless adults and children have participated in Dierbergs cooking classes, turned to Dierbergs *Everybody Cooks*® recipe magazine for fabulous food ideas and collected weekly recipes available in Dierbergs stores. For nearly two decades, Dierbergs' quarterly, prime-time, highly-rated *Everybody Cooks*® TV show has drawn a myriad of viewers. In 2004, Dierbergs School of Cooking published its first hardback cookbook, *The Best of Dierbergs, Treasured Recipes to Share with Family and Friends*. And now with this first in a series of topical cookbooks, it embarks on yet another exciting avenue in the world of food.

Dierbergs School of Cooking.
Good food. Good cooking. Good fun.

Enjoying Food and Wine

Food and wine are meant for each other. But deciding which wine to cook with or to serve can be a bit intimidating. Here are some things to keep in mind:

- Old Rule – Serve red wine with meat, white wine with fish and chicken. True, but very limiting. Red wines have bigger flavors and often taste better with heartier dishes. White wines tend to be more delicate and go better with milder-tasting chicken and fish entrées.

- New Rule – Don't dwell on the old rule! Today's dishes are less traditional and more inclined to have a variety of flavors, cooking methods and ethnic cuisines. There really isn't just one right match anymore. Follow your own sense of taste.

- Fruit is a flavor; sweetness is the level of sugar. Dry wines are low in sugar. Fruity wines have lots of fruit flavor. Just because a wine tastes *fruity* doesn't necessarily mean that it's *sweet*.

- Have fun tasting different wines! There's a wide range of flavor even within the same varietal wine. The only way to know which ones you enjoy is to sample them.

- Cooking with wine – See sidebar on page 47.

Storing and Serving Wine

- Store or rack wine horizontally in a dark, shaded space. This keeps the base of the cork moist, which seals the bottle properly and helps preserve the wine.

- Cool, moderate temperatures (50° to 60° F) are best for storing most wines. A wine refrigerator is best, but a cool basement can be a good alternative. Use the refrigerator to chill wine, but don't store wine in it. The lower humidity will dry out the cork. Ninety-nine percent of all wines are best served within a couple years of bottling.

- For the perfect serving temperature, chill white wines overnight in the refrigerator, taking them out a few minutes before you serve them. Chill red wines for just 40 minutes before serving.

- Once opened, enjoy wines within 24 hours. They keep a little longer if refrigerated. Let red wines come to room temperature before drinking.

Read The Label

Vintage – Younger wines have greater intensity, older wines gain depth and complexity, up to a point.

Varietal – If given a varietal name (Chardonnay or Merlot, for example), the bottle must contain at least 75 percent of that variety of grapes.

Place of origin – A very specific location says the producer is proud of the vineyard. (California, Monterey, Santa Lucia Highlands, West Terrace Vineyard, Block 7.)

Producer – Who made the wine? Have you enjoyed their wines in the past?

Alcohol content – The lower the alcohol content, the sweeter the wine.

Popular Red Wines
(lightest to most full-bodied)

Pinot Noir
Merlot
Shiraz (Syrah)
Zinfandel
Cabernet Sauvignon

Popular White Wines
(driest to sweetest)

Pinot Grigio (Pinot Gris)
Sauvignon Blanc
Fume Blanc
Chardonnay
Gewürztraminer
Riesling

Nutrition Information

Dierbergs Markets along with Missouri Baptist Medical Center, a member of BJC HealthCare, proudly sponsor *Eat Hearty*®, an informational program aimed at helping you choose a heart-healthy eating plan. In *Entrées*, you'll find heart-healthy recipes identified by the red heart logo 💙 shown with the nutrition analysis.

Recipes in this cookbook that have a red heart logo 💙 do not exceed 10 grams fat and 960 milligrams sodium per serving. (Several recipes containing salmon have slightly more than 10 grams of fat. The fat in salmon is rich in Omega-3 fatty acids, thus providing health benefits.) Sodium levels are a suggested level only. If you are following a sodium-restricted diet, please consult your physician or dietitian for specific recommendations.

Criteria Used for Calculating Nutrition Information

- Wherever a choice is given, the following are used: The first ingredient; the lesser amount of an ingredient; the larger number of servings.

- Ingredients without specific amounts listed, such as "optional," or "toppings," have not been included in the analysis.

- The nutrition information provided in *Entrées* was calculated using *Nutritionist Pro*, a nutrition analysis program developed by First DataBank, Inc. for The Hearst Corporation. The information is believed to be reliable and correct.

- The nutrition professionals compiling the information have made every effort to present the most accurate information available, but have undertaken no independent examination, investigation or verification of information provided by original sources. Therefore, Dierbergs assumes no liability and denies any responsibility for incorrect information resulting from the use of the nutrition information provided in *Entrées*.

Ingredients Used in Nutrition Calculations

- Certain ingredients are considered "standard" for nutrition analysis. They include large eggs, 2% milk, lean ground beef and canned broth. Other ingredient selections were based on information from the USDA and/or readily available brands.

- If a recipe specifies reduced-fat/reduced-sodium products in the ingredient list, these products were used for nutrition analysis.

- Some recipes meet *Eat Hearty* criteria without modification. You may wish to make additional substitutions to further reduce the fat/sodium content of these recipes.

Recipe Standards

The recipes in this cookbook were tested using the following standards unless otherwise indicated:

Eggs are large.

Butter is unsalted. Stick margarine may be substituted; do not substitute whipped butter, butter spreads or soft margarines.

Milk is 2% or higher fat; using fat-free or low-fat may alter results.

Dairy Products are regular or light/reduced-fat; using fat-free may alter results unless indicated in the recipe.

Vegetable Oil is your favorite brand.

Olive Oil is virgin.

Flour is all-purpose.

Brown Sugar is firmly packed when measured.

Coarse Salt is kosher or sea salt.

Pepper is ground black.

Preheat Oven for 10 minutes before beginning to cook.

How Many Cooks?

How many cooks does it take to develop just one Dierbergs recipe? Well, more than you would guess! Why? Because each recipe is carefully developed, tested and scrutinized with a seven-step process by Dierbergs (very picky) home economists and critiqued by a (very willing) taste panel. And our taste panel isn't shy in the area of feedback! We get many honest opinions with their diverse, discriminating palates. Foolproof recipes? You bet! We've done all the cooking and baking and testing and tasting. The results are wonderfully successful and wonderfully delicious.

entrées

Chicken Breasts with Wild Mushroom Stuffing
Recipe on page 12

Chicken Breasts with Wild Mushroom Stuffing

Home Economist Sally Bruns creates delicious menus for her classes on entertaining with ease. Her recipe for chicken breasts with a rich pancetta and shiitake mushroom filling will certainly give your guests something to talk about.

4 slices white bread
2 tablespoons chopped
  fresh parsley
4 ounces thinly sliced
  pancetta, chopped
1 medium onion, finely
  chopped
1/4 pound shiitake
  mushrooms, stemmed
  and chopped
3/4 cup shredded asiago
  cheese
6 large boneless, skinless
  chicken breast halves
2 eggs
2 tablespoons flour
1/2 teaspoon salt
1/4 teaspoon ground black
  pepper
2 to 4 tablespoons olive oil
  (divided)

In work bowl of food processor fitted with steel knife blade, process bread to form crumbs. Spread crumbs on baking sheet. Bake in 350° F oven stirring once until golden, about 4 to 6 minutes. Cool. In shallow dish, combine bread crumbs and parsley; set aside.

Heat large oven-proof skillet over medium-high heat. Add pancetta, onion and mushrooms; cook stirring occasionally until liquid evaporates, about 8 minutes. Transfer to bowl and cool. Stir in cheese.

1 To make pockets, insert tip of sharp knife into thicker side of each breast, about 1/2 inch from one end. Create pocket by slicing to within about 1/4 inch of the other side. **2** Stuff each breast with 1/4 of the mushroom mixture, distributing it evenly throughout pocket. Gently press to close pocket. In shallow dish, beat eggs with 2 tablespoons water. In second shallow dish, combine flour, salt and pepper. Coat chicken with flour mixture and dip into egg mixture; coat both sides with bread crumb mixture.

Wipe out inside of skillet with paper towel. Heat 1 tablespoon of the olive oil over medium-high heat. Add chicken; cook until golden brown, about 3 minutes per side, adding remaining oil as needed. Bake in 350° F oven until internal temperature of chicken and filling is 165° F, about 15 to 18 minutes.

Makes 6 servings

Per serving

Calories 494
Fat 22 g
Cholesterol 197 mg
Sodium 834 mg
Carbohydrate 13 g
Fiber 1 g

Photograph on page 10

Chicken Oscar

Chicken gets dressed for company! A luscious crab and béarnaise sauce and tender asparagus spears make this just right for a special occasion.

4 boneless, skinless chicken
  breast halves (about
  1 pound), lightly pounded
  to even thickness
2 tablespoons flour
½ teaspoon salt
½ teaspoon ground black
  pepper
1 to 2 tablespoons olive oil
1 cup dry white wine or
  chicken broth
1 large clove garlic, minced
1 package (0.9 ounce)
  béarnaise sauce mix, OR
  1 package (1.25 ounces)
  hollandaise sauce mix
1 can (6.5 ounces) white
  crab meat, drained and
  flaked
2 tablespoons lemon juice
1 pound asparagus,
  trimmed

On sheet of waxed paper, combine flour, salt and pepper. Lightly coat both sides of each chicken breast with seasoned flour. In large nonstick skillet, heat oil over medium-high heat. Add chicken; cook until browned and internal temperature of chicken is 165° F, about 3 to 4 minutes per side. Remove chicken from skillet; set aside.

Add wine and garlic to skillet; stir to scrape browned bits from bottom of pan. Cook until reduced to ¼ cup, about 5 minutes. Return chicken to skillet along with any accumulated juice; turn chicken to coat with sauce. Cook just until heated through.

Meanwhile, prepare béarnaise sauce according to package directions; stir in crab and lemon juice. Place asparagus in microwave-safe dish. Cover and microwave (high) for 4 minutes until crisp-tender.

Place one chicken breast on each of 4 serving plates. Top with sauce and asparagus.

Makes 4 servings

TIP If desired, use recipe for Béarnaise Sauce (recipe on page 90) in place of sauce mix.

cuisine savvy

Chicken Oscar

Chicken Oscar pays homage to its namesake, Veal Oscar. Legend states that Sweden's King Oscar II was very fond of this dish topped with crab meat, classic béarnaise sauce and tender asparagus spears. No wonder! They are flavors certainly fit for a king!

Per serving with sauce

Calories 369
Fat 20 g
Cholesterol 106 mg
Sodium 969 mg
Carbohydrate 12 g
Fiber 1 g

Chicken with Spinach and Artichokes

Many of Staff Home Economist Jeannie Rader's cooking classes focused on delectable entrées designed for stylish entertaining. This is one of her most requested recipes.

technique savvy

Temperature Check

Taking the temperature of thinner cuts of meat can be tricky. Thermometers inserted from the top may go all the way through the meat. For an accurate reading, insert the thermometer about 1-inch into the side of the boneless chicken breast rather than through the top. Chicken is done when the temperature registers 165° F on an instant-read thermometer.

6 boneless, skinless chicken breast halves (about 1½ pounds), lightly pounded to even thickness
Coarse salt and ground white pepper to taste
3 tablespoons olive oil
1 can (14 ounces) artichoke hearts, drained and chopped
1 package (10 ounces) fresh spinach, chopped
2 tablespoons butter
2 shallots, finely chopped
2 large cloves garlic, minced
1 cup chicken broth
¼ cup heavy whipping cream
1 ounce (¼ cup) crumbled blue cheese

Season each chicken breast with salt and pepper. In large nonstick skillet, heat oil over medium-high heat. Add chicken; cook until browned and internal temperature of chicken is 165° F, about 3 to 4 minutes per side. Remove chicken from skillet; cover and keep warm.

Add artichokes to same skillet; cook for 2 minutes. Add spinach; stir to combine. Reduce heat, cover and cook until spinach is wilted, about 2 to 3 minutes. Season with salt to taste; set aside.

In medium skillet, melt butter over medium-high heat. Add shallots and garlic; cook until softened, about 1 to 2 minutes. Add broth; cook until reduced by one-half, about 4 to 5 minutes. Add cream; cook until heated through, about 1 to 2 minutes. Reduce heat and stir in blue cheese until melted. Divide spinach mixture among 6 serving plates. Place chicken on top. Drizzle some of the sauce over chicken. Serve with remaining sauce. If desired, garnish with additional crumbled blue cheese.

Makes 6 servings

TIP If desired, substitute dry white wine for ½ cup of the chicken broth.

Per serving with sauce

Calories 264
Fat 17 g
Cholesterol 71 mg
Sodium 608 mg
Carbohydrate 7 g
Fiber 4 g

Raspberry Chipotle Chicken

Hot, spicy dishes are Staff Home Economist Therese Lewis' signature. Here is one of her favorites.

technique savvy

Pounding Chicken Breasts

Many recipes call for boneless, skinless chicken breasts pounded to an even thickness. This helps them cook more quickly and evenly, so watch cooking times carefully. To keep counters and utensils clean as you pound, slip a few chicken breasts at a time into a large freezer-weight plastic bag. Close but do not seal. Carefully pound them with the smooth side of a meat mallet to the desired thickness.

6 boneless, skinless chicken breast halves (about 1½ pounds), lightly pounded to even thickness
3 tablespoons fresh lime juice
1 teaspoon coarse salt
½ teaspoon coarsely ground black pepper
1 cup seedless raspberry jam
1 cup fresh or frozen raspberries
¼ cup dry red wine or balsamic vinegar
1 to 2 tablespoons puréed chipotle chiles in adobo sauce

Place chicken on platter. Drizzle with lime juice and sprinkle with salt and pepper; set aside.

In small saucepan, combine jam, raspberries, wine and chipotle purée; bring to a boil over medium-high heat. Reduce heat and simmer until slightly thickened, about 7 minutes. Remove ½ cup sauce for basting; reserve remaining raspberry sauce.

Place chicken on oiled grid over medium-high heat; grill brushing occasionally with basting sauce until internal temperature is 165° F, about 3 to 4 minutes per side. Discard any remaining basting sauce. Serve chicken with reserved raspberry sauce.

Makes 6 servings

TIP See Chipotle in Adobo Sauce information on page 62.

Per serving

Calories 241
Fat 1 g
Cholesterol 43 mg
Sodium 391 mg
Carbohydrate 39 g
Fiber 2 g

Chicken and Prosciutto Spiedini

Carol Ziemann is the food stylist for Dierbergs Presents Everybody Cooks® *TV show and a popular School of Cooking instructor. These savory prosciutto-stuffed chicken skewers are one of her favorite entrées for entertaining.*

4 boneless, skinless chicken
   breast halves (about
   1 pound)
²/₃ cup dry bread crumbs
¹/₃ cup grated parmesan
   cheese
¹/₂ teaspoon dried basil
¹/₂ teaspoon dried oregano
¹/₂ teaspoon garlic powder
¹/₄ teaspoon salt
2 tablespoons butter,
   melted
2 tablespoons extra virgin
   olive oil
8 thin slices prosciutto

Place chicken between sheets of plastic wrap; lightly pound to about ¼-inch thickness. On sheet of waxed paper, combine bread crumbs, cheese, basil, oregano, garlic powder and salt. In shallow dish, combine butter and olive oil. Dip each piece of chicken into butter mixture; coat both sides with crumb mixture. Top each chicken piece with 2 slices prosciutto; tightly roll up each piece. Cut into 1-inch-thick slices; thread onto skewers.

Place skewers on oiled grid over medium-high heat; grill until chicken is cooked through and coating is lightly browned, about 5 minutes per side.

Makes 4 servings

ingredient savvy

Prosciutto

Prosciutto (pro-SHOO-toh) is an Italian ham that has been cured and air-dried but not smoked. Prosciutto is ready to eat and traditionally served as an appetizer, often wrapped around wedges of cantaloupe or honeydew. It may also be added to recipes near the end of cooking time for a rich, salty accent. Purchase it sliced-to-order at Dierbergs Deli counter, or thinly sliced in packages in the self-serve section.

Per serving

Calories 330
Fat 18 g
Cholesterol 77 mg
Sodium 901 mg
Carbohydrate 14 g
Fiber 1 g

Lemon Ginger Chicken Salad

Classic chicken salad gets a new twist with the refreshing combination of lemon and fresh ginger.

technique savvy

How to Microwave Chicken

When a recipe calls for cooked chicken, cook it in the microwave! Place boneless, skinless chicken breasts in a microwave-safe dish. Cover with plastic wrap and vent to let steam escape. Microwave on high for 6 minutes per pound, rearranging pieces halfway through cooking time. Let stand for 5 minutes. The internal temperature should be 165° F. Add another minute or two of cooking if needed.

1½ pounds boneless, skinless chicken breast halves, cooked and cubed (about 3 cups)
1 cup thinly sliced celery
½ cup sweetened dried cranberries
⅓ cup light mayonnaise
2 teaspoons grated lemon peel
3 tablespoons fresh lemon juice
1 tablespoon minced fresh ginger root
1 tablespoon honey
Lemon wedges (optional)
¼ cup snipped fresh parsley (optional)

In large bowl, combine chicken, celery and dried cranberries. In small bowl, combine mayonnaise, lemon peel and juice, ginger and honey. Add to chicken; toss to coat. Cover and chill several hours or overnight. Serve on lettuce-lined plates. If desired, garnish with lemon wedges and snipped parsley.

Makes 6 servings

Per serving

Calories 204
Fat 7 g
Cholesterol 61 mg
Sodium 390 mg
Carbohydrate 14 g
Fiber <1 g

Roasted Chicken with Orange Rosemary Pan Sauce

Crispy roasted chicken scented with orange and rosemary will turn your dining room into a bistro.

1 whole roasting chicken
  (6 to 8 pounds)
2 small oranges
2 cloves garlic
Fresh rosemary sprigs
1 tablespoon olive oil
½ teaspoon salt
¼ teaspoon crushed red
  pepper flakes
3 tablespoons flour
1 cup chicken broth

Remove and discard giblets from chicken cavity. Place chicken on rack in shallow roasting pan.

Grate peel from 1 of the oranges (about 2 teaspoons); set aside. Cut oranges in half; squeeze 2 halves over chicken. Place remaining 2 orange halves inside chicken cavity along with garlic and several sprigs fresh rosemary. Roast in 375° F oven for 1 hour.

Meanwhile, strip 1 tablespoon rosemary leaves from stems; coarsely chop. In small bowl, combine chopped rosemary, reserved orange peel, olive oil, salt and red pepper flakes. Brush some of the mixture over surface of chicken. Continue roasting, basting occasionally with oil mixture, until internal temperature of breast meat is 170° F, about 30 minutes to 1 hour (about 1½ to 2 hours total roasting time). Cover and let stand 10 minutes before carving.

Skim fat from pan drippings. Place pan with drippings over medium heat; stir to scrape browned bits from bottom of pan. In small bowl, whisk flour into chicken broth. Add to pan drippings. Cook stirring occasionally until mixture begins to boil and thicken. Serve with chicken.

Makes 6-8 servings

ingredient savvy

Citrus Zest

Citrus fruit adds a little sunshine to all sorts of recipes. The *zest*, or colored portion of the peel, contains fragrant oils that are loaded with flavor. Finely grate just the zest, stopping when you reach the white pith beneath, which tends to be bitter. Once the zest has been removed, cut the fruit and squeeze the juice, or store the fruit in a plastic bag in the refrigerator for several days for other uses.

Per serving with sauce and without skin

Calories 229
Fat 6 g
Cholesterol 113 mg
Sodium 370 mg
Carbohydrate 5 g
Fiber <1 g

Cornish Hens with Mustard Sauce

Staff Home Economist Nancy Lorenz gets her recipe inspiration from the many different cultures of her hometown in Winnipeg, Manitoba. Her elegant Cornish hens are a very special entrée for company.

ingredient savvy

Cornish Hens

Sometimes called *game hens*, these miniature chickens make a lovely presentation for a special meal. Cornish hens are available frozen and range from 1 to 2 pounds. For hens weighing 1 pound, plan on 1 hen per person. For larger hens, plan on 1/2 hen per person.

2 frozen Cornish hens (about 1 1/2 pounds each), thawed and cut in half
1/2 cup butter, melted
1/2 cup Dijon-style mustard
2 tablespoons honey
2 tablespoons fresh lemon juice
2 tablespoons minced garlic
2 tablespoons fresh thyme
2 teaspoons coarse salt
1/2 teaspoon ground black pepper
2/3 cup dry white wine
1/3 cup chicken broth
1 tablespoon cornstarch, dissolved in 1 tablespoon water
Wild Rice Pancakes

Place hens in large freezer-weight reclosable plastic bag. In small bowl, stir together butter, mustard, honey, lemon juice, garlic, thyme, salt and pepper. Pour half of the mixture over hens; reserve remaining mixture for basting. Seal bag and turn to coat hens. Place bag on plate and marinate in refrigerator for 4 hours.

Remove hens from bag; discard marinade. Place hens skin-side down on rack of broiler pan. Broil hens 6 inches from heat source for 20 minutes. Turn hens skin-side up and brush with some of the reserved butter mixture. Broil until internal temperature of breast is 165° F, about 10 to 15 minutes.

Place remaining butter mixture, wine and broth in small saucepan. Bring to a boil; cook for 5 minutes. Pour pan drippings into wine mixture. Stir in cornstarch mixture. Cook stirring constantly until slightly thickened, about 1 minute. Serve hens with sauce and Wild Rice Pancakes.

Makes 4 servings

Wild Rice Pancakes

2 cups cooked wild rice
1/4 cup minced red onion
2 eggs, separated
2 tablespoons flour
1 teaspoon fresh thyme
1/2 teaspoon coarse salt
1/4 teaspoon ground black pepper
1 to 2 tablespoons vegetable oil

In medium bowl, combine wild rice, onion, egg yolks, flour, thyme, salt and pepper. In medium bowl, beat egg whites until stiff peaks form. Fold into rice mixture. Heat large skillet over medium heat; add oil. Spoon batter into hot skillet in 4 equal portions. Cook until set and lightly browned, about 3 minutes per side.

Makes 4 servings

Per 1/2 hen with 1 pancake

Calories 520
Fat 24 g
Cholesterol 265 mg
Sodium 1349 mg
Carbohydrate 34 g
Fiber 1 g

Turkey Medallions with Caramelized Onion Cider Sauce

This quick and easy recipe is perfect for a busy weeknight supper. Cider adds a mellow sweetness to the sauce.

ingredient savvy

Turkey Tenderloins

Turkey tenderloins are great any time of year. Cut from the center of the turkey breast, this boneless, skinless cut typically weighs 8 to 16 ounces. Marinate turkey tenderloins and grill over direct heat, or slice into 1-inch-thick pieces and sauté for about 4 minutes per side. Turkey is done when it reaches an internal temperature of 165° F and the juices are no longer pink.

1½ to 2 pounds turkey tenderloin
2 tablespoons flour
¼ teaspoon salt
¼ teaspoon ground black pepper
2 tablespoons olive oil (divided)
2 cups chopped onion
1 clove garlic, minced
1 teaspoon dried thyme
1 cup chicken broth
¾ cup apple cider

Slice tenderloins into 1-inch-thick medallions; flatten slightly with heel of hand. On sheet of waxed paper, combine flour, salt and pepper. Coat both sides of medallions with flour mixture, shaking off excess. Reserve remaining flour mixture.

In large skillet, heat 1 tablespoon of the olive oil over medium-high heat. Add medallions; cook until no longer pink, about 2 to 3 minutes per side. Transfer meat to platter; cover to keep warm.

Place skillet with drippings over medium heat. Add remaining 1 tablespoon of olive oil, onion and garlic; cook stirring occasionally until onions are golden brown and caramelized, about 7 minutes. Stir in reserved flour mixture and thyme; cook for 1 minute. Whisk in broth and apple cider. Bring to a boil; cook stirring occasionally until slightly thickened, about 5 minutes. Serve sauce over medallions.

Makes 4-6 servings

Per serving

Calories 210
Fat 6 g
Cholesterol 60 mg
Sodium 315 mg
Carbohydrate 12 g
Fiber 1 g

Sage Roasted Turkey Breast with Shallot and Mushroom Stuffing

Fresh sage leaves tucked under the skin flavor the turkey as it roasts.

technique savvy

Removing Rib Bones

To remove back and rib bones from turkey breast, use sharp knife and cut through small rib bones. This allows breast to sit more securely during roasting. Bones may be used to make turkey stock.

1 whole turkey breast
   (6 to 8 pounds), thawed
   if frozen
10 large sage leaves
3 shallots, sliced
2 tablespoons fresh thyme,
   OR 2 teaspoons dried
   thyme
1 tablespoon slivered fresh
   sage leaves
¼ cup olive oil
2 cups sliced cremini
   mushrooms (about
   8 ounces)
1 cup stemmed and sliced
   shiitake mushrooms
   (about 4 ounces)
½ cup dry Marsala wine or
   dry sherry
1 teaspoon ground black
   pepper
1 bag (12 to 14 ounces)
   herb-seasoned stuffing
   cubes
1 can (14 ounces) low-
   sodium chicken broth

Rinse turkey, removing back/rib bones, if desired (see sidebar). Carefully loosen skin and place 5 sage leaves under skin on each side of turkey. Pull skin tightly back in place; secure with wooden picks.

In small, shallow ovenproof dish, combine shallots, thyme and sage. Drizzle with olive oil; toss to coat. Roast in 375° F oven stirring once until shallots are tender, about 25 minutes. Reserve 1 tablespoon of the oil to baste turkey breast.

In large skillet, combine mushrooms, wine and pepper. Simmer stirring occasionally until mushrooms soften, about 10 to 15 minutes. In large bowl, combine stuffing cubes, shallot mixture, mushroom mixture and chicken broth. Place in 9x13-inch baking dish that has been coated with no-stick cooking spray. Place turkey breast on top of stuffing. Brush part of the reserved oil over turkey. Roast in 325° F oven for 1 hour. Brush remaining oil over turkey. Roast until internal temperature in thickest part of breast is 165° F, about 2½ to 3 hours total cooking time. Loosely cover with foil during last hour of cooking to prevent over-browning. Cover and let stand 10 minutes before slicing.

Makes 12-16 servings

Per serving without skin

Calories 277
Fat 5 g
Cholesterol 88 mg
Sodium 420 mg
Carbohydrate 18 g
Fiber 1 g

Roasted Turkey with Chardonnay Sauce

Brining keeps the turkey moist and juicy. The silky Chardonnay Sauce adds an elegant touch.

1 whole turkey breast
(6 to 8 pounds), thawed
if frozen
3 tablespoons butter, at
room temperature
(divided)
¼ cup flour
½ cup Chardonnay wine
½ teaspoon herbes de
Provence
1 can (14 ounces) low-
sodium chicken broth
(divided)

Brine non-basted turkey according to directions, if desired (see recipe).

Place turkey on rack in shallow roasting pan. Loosen skin; rub 2 tablespoons of the butter under skin and over top of turkey. Roast in 350° F oven until internal temperature in thickest part of breast is 165° F (see package directions for roasting times). Place turkey on cutting board; cover loosely with foil for at least 10 minutes before slicing.

Pour drippings into 1-cup glass measure. Skim 2 tablespoons fat from drippings and return fat to pan along with remaining 1 tablespoon butter. Skim and discard remaining fat from drippings; reserve drippings. Stir flour into pan; cook until lightly browned. Add wine and herbes de Provence; stir to scrape browned bits from bottom of pan. Cook until slightly reduced. Whisk in broth and reserved drippings. Bring to a boil; cook until thickened, about 3 minutes. Remove from heat. If desired, add splash of Chardonnay to sauce. Serve turkey with sauce.

Makes 12-16 servings and about 2 cups sauce

TIP For dynamic flavor, substitute Dierbergs Chardonnay Shallot Herb Butter for plain butter and herbes de Provence.

Brine for Turkey Breast

8 cups cold water
2 tablespoons brown sugar
½ cup coarse salt
2 bay leaves
1 tablespoon whole allspice
1 tablespoon whole cloves

Place turkey breast in freezer-weight 2-gallon reclosable plastic bag; place in deep 6-quart bowl, meat-side down. In 2-quart batter bowl, combine brine ingredients; stir until sugar and salt dissolve. Pour over turkey in bag. Seal bag; refrigerate for 8 hours. Remove turkey from brine; discard brine and whole spices. Pat dry and cook as directed.

ingredient savvy

Self-basting Turkey

Before you brine a turkey, check the label. Many frozen turkeys are *self-basting*, which means they have been injected with a salt solution to help keep the meat moist. Do not brine a self-basting turkey; it will result in meat that is too salty.

Per serving without skin or brine

Calories 190
Fat 5 g
Cholesterol 95 mg
Sodium 130 mg
Carbohydrate 2 g
Fiber <1 g

BEEF
entrées

Crab-Stuffed Beef Tenderloin with Jack Daniel's Sauce
Recipe on page 28

Crab-Stuffed Beef Tenderloin with Jack Daniel's Sauce

technique savvy

Step-by-step Instructions

Dazzle your guests with one of our most requested entrées. Beef tenderloin is wrapped around a luscious crab stuffing and served with Jack Daniel's Sauce. Need we say more?

1 center-cut beef tenderloin (about 2 pounds), trimmed
2 cloves garlic, minced
Salt and pepper to taste
1 cup spinach leaves, stems removed
1 jar (7 ounces) roasted red bell peppers, drained and patted dry
Crab Stuffing (recipe on page 29)
Kitchen twine
1 tablespoon olive oil
Seasoned pepper
Jack Daniel's Sauce (recipe on page 89)

Place very cold tenderloin on cutting board lined with sheet of plastic wrap. **1** Using large, sharp knife, make horizontal cut ½ inch from bottom of roast, cutting to within ½ inch of opposite edge. Roll tenderloin, exposing cut surface. Continue cutting and rolling until you have flat piece of meat (about 7x10 inches). Place another sheet of plastic wrap on top of meat. With meat mallet, lightly pound meat to an even ½-inch thickness (about 10x11 inches).

Remove top layer of plastic wrap. Rub garlic, salt and pepper over meat. Top with half of the spinach leaves, covering all but 2-inch strip on first-cut edge. Arrange roasted peppers over spinach in single layer. Spread chilled Crab Stuffing over peppers, leaving the 2-inch strip uncovered and spreading to within 1 inch of remaining edges. Top with remaining spinach leaves. **2** Roll up tenderloin jellyroll style toward first cut edge. **3** Tie with kitchen twine to hold together. (At this point, meat can be wrapped and refrigerated for up to 24 hours. Let stand at room temperature for 30 minutes before roasting.)

Rub outside of meat with olive oil and sprinkle with seasoned pepper. Place on rack in shallow roasting pan. Roast in 425° F oven until internal temperature is 135° F for medium-rare, about 50 to 55 minutes. Cover and let stand 15 minutes before slicing. Serve warm with Jack Daniel's Sauce.

Makes 6-8 servings

Photograph on page 26

Crab Stuffing for Tenderloin

2 tablespoons butter
1 large shallot, minced
1/4 cup finely chopped green
  bell pepper
1 can (6.5 ounces) white
  crab meat, drained
4 ounces (half of 8-ounce
  package) garlic and herb
  cream cheese, softened
1/4 teaspoon paprika
1/4 teaspoon salt
1/4 teaspoon ground white
  pepper

In medium skillet, melt butter over medium-high heat. Add shallot and bell pepper; cook until tender, about 3 minutes. Place in medium bowl. Stir in remaining ingredients. Refrigerate for at least 30 minutes.

Makes about 1 cup

technique savvy

Tie One On

A savory stuffing adds a delicious touch of class to a roast. To secure the goods and keep the tasty filling inside while the meat cooks, tie the roast together using heavy cotton kitchen twine made for this purpose. A package of unflavored, unwaxed dental floss does the job, too, and is easy to keep on hand.

**Per serving of beef
with stuffing and sauce**

Calories 498
Fat 38 g
Cholesterol 115 mg
Sodium 677 mg
Carbohydrate 5 g
Fiber 1 g

Beef Tenderloin with Roasted Vegetables

Sometimes a few simple ingredients are all it takes to create a memorable meal. Perfectly roasted beef and a savory vegetable medley couldn't be easier or more delicious.

ingredient savvy

Beef Tenderloin

It just doesn't get any better than beef tenderloin! A center-cut tenderloin will be very uniform in diameter. If one end of the roast is thinner, tuck it under and tie it with kitchen twine to form a more uniform shape. This assures even cooking. Because it is so lean, this special roast is best cooked quickly in a hot oven. For moist, tender beef, cook a tenderloin to no more than medium doneness.

3 tablespoons herbes de Provence
2 teaspoons salt
1 center-cut beef tenderloin (2½ to 3 pounds), trimmed
6 cloves garlic, slivered
2 red or yellow bell peppers, seeded and cut into 8 wedges
1 large red onion, cut into wedges
1½ pounds baby squash, OR 2 yellow squash and 2 zucchini, cut into 1-inch cubes
2 tablespoons olive oil

In small bowl, combine herbes de Provence and salt. Rub 3 tablespoons of the herb mixture over surface of tenderloin. Place in shallow roasting pan. Tuck garlic under meat so it is completely covered. Roast in 425° F oven until internal temperature is 135° F for medium-rare, about 35 to 45 minutes. Place beef on cutting board. Cover and let stand for 15 minutes before slicing.

In same roasting pan, combine vegetables with partially cooked garlic. Drizzle with olive oil; toss to coat. Sprinkle with remaining herb mixture. Roast uncovered in 425° F oven until vegetables are crisp-tender, about 12 to 16 minutes.

Slice tenderloin and serve with roasted vegetables.

Makes 8-10 servings

Per serving

Calories 186
Fat 10 g
Cholesterol 52 mg
Sodium 510 mg
Carbohydrate 5 g
Fiber 1 g

Barbecued Beef Brisket

This tender and delicious brisket is a Dierbergs classic. Coffee adds richness to the sauce and helps tenderize the meat.

1 flat-cut beef brisket
   (3 to 4 pounds)
1 cup ketchup
½ cup strong coffee
¼ cup firmly packed brown
   sugar
3 tablespoons lemon juice
1 tablespoon Worcestershire
   sauce
2 cloves garlic, minced

Trim and discard visible fat from beef. Place meat in shallow roasting pan. In small bowl, combine remaining ingredients; pour mixture over meat. Cover tightly and cook in 325° F oven until tender, about 3 to 3½ hours. Cool beef slightly before thinly slicing across the grain. Serve warm with sauce. Also makes delicious sandwiches.

Makes 6-8 servings

TIP Beef and sauce can be made a day ahead. Cover and refrigerate meat and sauce in separate containers. Skim fat from surface of sauce. To reheat, place meat and sauce in shallow baking pan. Cover and bake in 325° F oven until heated through.

ingredient savvy

Beef Brisket

You can't rush tenderness! A little patience goes a long way in delivering delicious results from this not-so-tender, yet very flavorful cut. Whether you choose *point-cut* (more fat) or *flat-cut* (less fat) brisket, trim away the excess fat. Brisket tastes best when braised – browned quickly on the outside, then slowly simmered in liquid for a few hours.

Per serving

Calories 503
Fat 35 g
Cholesterol 134 mg
Sodium 445 mg
Carbohydrate 16 g
Fiber <1 g

Garlic-Infused Standing Rib Roast

Few things are as grand as this "king of roasts." It's surprisingly simple to prepare and always gets rave reviews.

1 standing rib roast
  (6 to 8 pounds), chine
  bone removed
1 tablespoon coarse salt
1½ teaspoons dried thyme
½ teaspoon freshly ground
  black pepper
4 cloves garlic, slivered

Preheat oven to 450° F. With sharp knife, separate meat from bones, cutting close to ribs.

In small bowl, combine salt, thyme and pepper; sprinkle seasoning over bones and top of roast; spread garlic over bones. Replace meat on bones; tie in place.

Place roast bone-side down in 9x13-inch pan. Place in oven and *immediately* reduce oven temperature to 350° F. Roast until internal temperature is 130° F for medium, about 2 to 3 hours. Remove from oven and let stand covered until internal temperature is 145° F, about 15 to 30 minutes. Snip string; place meat on cutting board and slice.

Makes 6-8 servings

ingredient savvy

Standing Rib Roast

Standing rib roast, also known as prime rib, is a succulent roast worthy of special occasions. It comes with a built-in roasting rack – the rib bones! Placing the roast bone-side down keeps the meat off the bottom of the pan. This also allows the top layer of fat to melt over the roast as it cooks so you don't have to baste.

Per serving

Calories 306
Fat 14 g
Cholesterol 101 mg
Sodium 817 mg
Carbohydrate 1 g
Fiber <1 g

Mustard-Glazed Corned Beef with Horseradish Cream

A sweet and savory glaze takes corned beef from simple to sublime. The zesty Horseradish Cream is the perfect complement.

1 corned beef brisket
   (2 to 3 pounds)
½ cup chopped onion
2 cloves garlic
1 bay leaf
1 teaspoon whole black
   peppercorns
2 tablespoons Dijon-style
   mustard
3 tablespoons brown sugar
1 teaspoon paprika
Horseradish Cream

Place corned beef in large heavy pot or Dutch oven. Add enough water to barely cover meat. Add onion, garlic, bay leaf and peppercorns; cover and simmer until tender, about 3 to 4 hours. (Add water if necessary to keep meat covered.)

Remove meat from pot. Trim and discard fat. Place meat in shallow roasting pan. Spread mustard evenly over top of corned beef.

In small bowl, combine brown sugar and paprika; sprinkle evenly over mustard. Cook in 375° F oven until glazed, about 15 to 20 minutes. Cool slightly before slicing ¼-inch thick across the grain. Serve with Horseradish Cream.

Makes 4-6 servings

Horseradish Cream

½ cup heavy whipping
   cream
2 to 3 tablespoons prepared
   horseradish
Salt to taste

In small bowl with hand mixer, beat cream at high speed until stiff peaks form. Fold in horseradish; add salt to taste.

Makes about 1 cup

ingredient savvy

Corned Beef

Whether it's a brisket or a round, corned beef is cured in seasoned brine. The round is much leaner than the brisket. Slowly cook either one in liquid for tender, delicious results.

Per serving with
2 tablespoons cream

Calories 351
Fat 24 g
Cholesterol 97 mg
Sodium 1143 mg
Carbohydrate 11 g
Fiber <1 g

Oven-Braised Short Ribs

No need to call everyone to the dinner table...the heavenly aroma of these succulent beef ribs will do it for you!

ingredient savvy

Short Ribs

Beef short ribs are an old-fashioned cut made new again. Exactly what they sound like, these short pieces of rib are cut from anywhere along the rib section. English-style short ribs are individual bones with a thick chunk of meat attached. Flanken-style short ribs are cut into 2 to 3 rib sections. Slow braising takes time, but makes short ribs fall-off-the-bone tender with a rich, meaty sauce.

4 to 5 pounds bone-in beef short ribs
Salt and pepper to taste
2 cans (14 ounces each) reduced-sodium beef broth
1 cup dry red wine
¼ cup soy sauce
1 cup diced onion
½ cup diced carrot
½ cup diced celery
1 teaspoon dried thyme, crushed
1 bay leaf
⅓ cup flour
½ cup water

Trim and discard excess fat from short ribs; season meat with salt and pepper. Place on rack of broiler pan. Broil 4 inches from heat source until well browned, about 8 to 10 minutes per side.

In Dutch oven, combine remaining ingredients except flour and water. Add short ribs; cover and cook in 325° F oven until meat is very tender, about 2 to 2½ hours. Place meat on serving platter.

Skim fat from pan drippings; remove bay leaf. In small bowl, stir together flour and water; gradually stir into pan drippings. Cook over medium heat stirring frequently until thickened, about 5 minutes. Serve gravy with short ribs.

Makes 8 servings

TIP Short ribs are best prepared ahead. Refrigerate ribs and gravy separately. Skim fat from gravy. Heat gravy; add ribs. Cover and cook over low heat until heated through.

Per serving

Calories 211
Fat 8 g
Cholesterol 53 mg
Sodium 919 mg
Carbohydrate 8 g
Fiber 1 g

Company Pot Roast

A Sunday dinner favorite gets a makeover. Lean and flavorful eye of round and plenty of delicious gravy will have everyone asking for second helpings.

technique savvy

Braising

Braising is one of the best ways to make a less-tender cut, like eye of round, one of the most tender roasts you ever tasted. First, trim away any excess fat. Brown the roast in a skillet in a small amount of hot oil. Then transfer it to a heavy Dutch oven or roasting pan and add liquid – broth, wine or water – to come halfway up the sides of the roast. Cover tightly and simmer it slowly. You'll have a deliciously tender roast and lots of flavorful juices to serve alongside.

Per serving

Calories 208
Fat 9 g
Cholesterol 45 mg
Sodium 323 mg
Carbohydrate 6 g
Fiber 1 g

1 eye of round beef roast (about 2½ pounds)
1 small onion, finely chopped
2 carrots, finely chopped
2 ribs celery, finely chopped
1 clove garlic, minced
1 can (10.5 ounces) French onion soup
2 tablespoons tomato paste
2 tablespoons flour, dissolved in 2 tablespoons water

Trim and discard visible fat from meat; place meat in Dutch oven. In medium bowl, combine onion, carrots, celery and garlic; spoon over top of roast. Pour soup into pan. Cover and cook in 325° F oven until well done and tender, about 2½ hours.

Remove roast from pan; set aside. Add tomato paste to pan drippings. Stir in flour mixture. Cook over medium-high heat stirring frequently until sauce thickens slightly, about 2 to 3 minutes. Slice roast across the grain and serve warm with sauce.

Makes 10 servings

Peppered Beef

Perfect for parties and potlucks, this recipe has been a favorite of Dierbergs' customers for years. Serve it on crusty rolls for terrific roast beef sandwiches.

1 eye of round beef roast
   (about 2 1/2 pounds)
1/3 cup coarsely ground
   black pepper
3/4 cup soy sauce
1/4 cup lemon juice
1/4 cup prepared barbecue
   sauce
1 clove garlic, minced

Trim and discard visible fat from meat. Place pepper on sheet of waxed paper; firmly roll roast in pepper to cover all sides of meat. Place meat in large freezer-weight reclosable plastic bag. In small bowl, combine remaining ingredients. Pour over meat; seal bag and turn to coat meat. Place bag on plate; marinate in refrigerator for 4 to 5 hours or overnight.

Remove meat from bag and place on rack in shallow roasting pan; pour marinade over meat. Roast in 325° F oven, basting occasionally with pan juices, until internal temperature is 145° F for medium, about 1 1/2 to 2 hours. Place roast on cutting board. Cover and let stand for 10 minutes before slicing very thinly across the grain. Serve warm with pan sauce.

Makes 8-10 servings

technique savvy

Eye of Round

Eye of round is lean and flavorful. Even though it looks like beef tenderloin, it requires very different cooking. You can marinate the meat to tenderize and add extra flavor. Then cook the roast only to medium doneness – remember, it's lean and can dry out quickly. The other choice is to braise eye of round very slowly in a liquid, like our Company Pot Roast (page 38). Either way, slice it thinly across the grain and you're ready to enjoy.

Per serving

Calories 203
Fat 9 g
Cholesterol 48 mg
Sodium 461 mg
Carbohydrate 4 g
Fiber 1 g

Hazelnut-Crusted Steaks with Madeira Cherry Sauce

In a word, "Wow!" Tender steak with an elegant hazelnut crust and rich cherry sauce will surely impress your guests.

4 New York strip steaks
   (about 3/4 pound each)
Salt and pepper to taste
2 tablespoons butter
1/2 cup (2 ounces) chopped
   hazelnuts
2 tablespoons mayonnaise
2 large cloves garlic, minced
   (divided)
1/2 cup diced shallots
1 cup Madeira wine
1 tablespoon brown sugar
1 teaspoon dried tarragon
2 teaspoons cornstarch,
   dissolved in 1 tablespoon
   water
1 package (12 ounces)
   frozen dark sweet cherries,
   thawed

Season steaks with salt and pepper. In medium skillet, melt butter over medium-high heat. Cook steaks in batches until browned, about 2 minutes per side. Place in 9x13-inch baking dish that has been coated with no-stick cooking spray.

In small bowl, combine hazelnuts, mayonnaise and half of the minced garlic. Spread over steaks. Cook in 350° F oven until internal temperature is 145° F for medium, about 10 to 15 minutes.

In same skillet, cook shallots and remaining garlic for 1 minute. Add wine, brown sugar and tarragon. Bring to a boil; cook for 10 minutes. Stir cornstarch mixture into sauce and cook until thickened, about 1 to 2 minutes. Stir in cherries; cook until heated through. Serve sauce over steaks.

Makes 4 servings

ingredient savvy

Madeira Wine

Made on the Portuguese island of the same name, Madeira is a fortified wine, or one that has been enhanced with a bit of brandy or other spirit. Madeira's color ranges from pale to deep amber, and its flavor ranges from dry to very sweet. Use it in both sweet and savory dishes to add a deep, rich flavor.

Per serving with sauce

Calories 651
Fat 28 g
Cholesterol 136 mg
Sodium 174 mg
Carbohydrate 24 g
Fiber 3 g

Steak Mudega

Staff Home Economist Jennifer Kassel's creative cooking classes span the culinary spectrum from tempting appetizers to wine country classics. You'll love Jennifer's version of this restaurant-style steak.

cuisine savvy

Mudega

Mudega is Italian steak – St. Louis style, that is. Found on many restaurant menus in our fair city, steak gets the royal treatment with a coating of savory crumbs, a luscious wine sauce and a crowning touch of creamy melted cheese.

1 beef sirloin steak, (1½ to 2 pounds)
2 tablespoons olive oil
2 tablespoons dry sherry
2 cloves garlic, minced
½ teaspoon ground black pepper
⅔ cup Italian seasoned bread crumbs
½ cup provel cheese ropes
Mudega Sauce (recipe on page 88)

Trim and discard visible fat from meat. Cut meat into 6 serving-sized pieces. Place meat in large freezer-weight reclosable plastic bag. In small bowl, stir together olive oil, sherry, garlic and pepper. Pour over meat; seal bag and turn to coat meat. Place bag on plate; marinate in refrigerator for at least 30 minutes or up to several hours.

Remove meat from bag; discard marinade. Place bread crumbs on sheet of waxed paper; coat both sides of meat with crumbs. Place on rack of foil-lined broiler pan. Broil 4 inches from heat source until internal temperature is 145° F for medium, about 6 minutes per side.

Top each piece of meat with cheese. Broil until cheese is bubbly, about 2 minutes. Serve warm with sauce.

Makes 6 servings

Per serving with 2 tablespoons sauce

Calories 358
Fat 14 g
Cholesterol 119 mg
Sodium 589 mg
Carbohydrate 11 g
Fiber 1 g

Mandarin Orange Beef

Certified Culinary Professional and St. Louis Post-Dispatch *columnist, Mary Billings has been an instructor at Dierbergs School of Cooking since 1988. Chinese cuisine, including this delicious stir-fry, is one of her specialties.*

3 large oranges
2 tablespoons cornstarch
1½ pounds beef breakfast steaks, cut into 1-inch squares
3 to 4 cloves garlic, minced
3 tablespoons sugar
3 tablespoons soy sauce
1 tablespoon grated fresh ginger root
1 bunch green onions, white parts sliced, and green parts cut into 1-inch pieces
2 tablespoons peanut oil

Remove wide strips of zest from one of the oranges and set strips aside for garnish. Grate 2 tablespoons zest from remaining oranges; squeeze juice from all 3 oranges.

In large bowl, combine grated orange zest, 2 tablespoons of the orange juice and cornstarch. Add beef and toss to coat; marinate for 10 to 15 minutes.

In small bowl, stir together ¾ cup of the orange juice, garlic, sugar, soy sauce, ginger and white part of the green onions; set aside.

Heat large nonstick skillet over high heat. Add oil and meat; spread meat out in skillet and allow to brown before stirring. Toss and continue to cook until most of the pink has disappeared. Add orange juice mixture and cook until sauce reaches the consistency of gravy, about 4 to 5 minutes. Stir in green part of green onions and wide strips of orange zest. Serve hot with steamed rice.

Makes 6 servings

ingredient savvy

Breakfast Steaks

Like many cuts of meat, Breakfast Steaks can have a different name depending on where you live. Finding what you want can be like reading aliases on a *Most Wanted* poster! Breakfast Steaks – a.k.a. Sandwich Steaks or Minute Steaks – are cut from the round tip or leg area. They are usually cut ⅛- to ¼-inch thick, making them perfect for quick-cooking recipes like a stir-fry.

Per serving

Calories 242
Fat 10 g
Cholesterol 69 mg
Sodium 525 mg
Carbohydrate 12 g
Fiber 1 g

entrées

Honey Balsamic-Glazed Pork with Roasted Vegetables
Recipe on page 46

Honey Balsamic-Glazed Pork with Roasted Vegetables

Make a grand impression at your holiday feast with this succulent roast. Colorful vegetables are the perfect partner.

ingredient savvy

Balsamic Vinegar

A splash of smooth and mellow balsamic vinegar brightens everything from salads to sauces to even desserts. This popular Italian vinegar is made from white Trebbiano grape juice. Its characteristic deep caramel color and sweetness come from years of aging in wooden barrels. For a special treat, drizzle a little balsamic vinegar over sliced fresh strawberries. The berries are terrific alone or over vanilla ice cream.

1 bone-in pork loin roast (loin half) (6 to 7 pounds)
2 teaspoons salt
1 teaspoon ground black pepper
1 teaspoon rubbed sage
1 bag (32 ounces) baby carrots
10 shallots, peeled (halved, if large)
2 pounds fresh fennel
1/2 cup honey
1/4 cup balsamic vinegar
1 1/2 tablespoons olive oil

Place roast bone-side down in shallow roasting pan. In small bowl, combine salt, pepper and sage; rub over surface of pork. Roast in 350° F oven for 1 hour.

Meanwhile, in large bowl, combine carrots and shallots. Trim and discard stems from fennel. Cut bulbs in half lengthwise and remove core. Slice fennel into 1-inch pieces; add to carrots.

In small bowl, stir together honey and vinegar. Toss vegetables with 3 tablespoons of the honey mixture and the olive oil. Arrange vegetables in roasting pan around pork. Roast, basting pork and vegetables occasionally with remaining honey mixture, until internal temperature of pork is 155° F, an additional 1 to 1 1/2 hours (2 to 2 1/2 hours total cooking time).

Cover roast and let stand 10 minutes before slicing. Place on serving platter with vegetables.

Makes 8 servings

TIP See Fresh Fennel information on page 80.

Per 3-ounce cooked portion

Calories 280
Fat 10 g
Cholesterol 69 mg
Sodium 486 mg
Carbohydrate 22 g
Fiber 3 g

Photograph on page 44

Maple Orange-Glazed Pork Roast with Cornbread Stuffing

A zesty orange marinade and a drizzle of pure maple syrup make this roast something special. Serve it alongside Cornbread Stuffing for a terrific Sunday supper.

1 boneless center-cut pork loin roast (about 2 pounds)
2 teaspoons freshly grated orange peel
1/3 cup fresh orange juice
1/4 cup dry white wine (optional)
1/4 cup pure maple syrup
Cornbread Stuffing

Trim and discard visible fat from pork. Place roast in large freezer-weight reclosable plastic bag. In small bowl, stir together orange peel, juice and wine. Pour over meat; seal bag and turn to coat meat. Place bag on plate; marinate in refrigerator for several hours or overnight.

Remove roast from bag and place on rack in shallow roasting pan. Drizzle several tablespoons of the marinade over meat; discard remaining marinade. Roast in 350° F oven for 15 minutes. Baste with maple syrup. Continue roasting, basting occasionally with syrup, until internal temperature is 155° F, about 35 to 45 minutes (50 to 60 minutes total cooking time).

Cover and let stand for 10 minutes before slicing. Serve with Cornbread Stuffing.

Makes 6-8 servings

Cornbread Stuffing

1 package (16 ounces) cornbread stuffing crumbs
1 small onion, chopped
2 ribs celery, thinly sliced
1/2 cup chopped fresh parsley
1 to 2 teaspoons freshly grated orange peel
1/4 teaspoon ground black pepper
1 can (14 ounces) chicken broth
2/3 cup water
2 tablespoons butter, melted

In large bowl, combine stuffing crumbs, onion, celery and parsley. Sprinkle orange peel and pepper over stuffing. Drizzle broth, water and butter over stuffing; toss until evenly mixed. Place in 2-quart baking dish that has been coated with no-stick cooking spray. Cover and bake in 350° F oven for 30 minutes. Remove cover and bake an additional 15 minutes.

Makes 6-8 servings

ingredient savvy

Wine for Cooking

Confused about which wines to cook with? It's fairly simple: If you can drink it, you can cook with it. For savory dishes, choose dry (not sweet) wines. Dry white wines include Chardonnay, Pinot Grigio and Sauvignon Blanc. Dry red wines like Cabernet Sauvignon, Chianti, Merlot, Pinot Noir, Burgundy and Shiraz are good choices. Avoid products labeled *cooking wine*. They contain salt, which can alter the flavor of the recipe.

Per serving with stuffing

Calories 390
Fat 9 g
Cholesterol 55 mg
Sodium 883 mg
Carbohydrate 52 g
Fiber 3 g

Spinach-Stuffed Pork Loin with Brandy Sauce

A ribbon of savory spinach stuffing flavors each slice of this tender roast. The rich brandy sauce adds an elegant touch.

ingredient savvy

Shallots

Shallots, like onion and garlic, are part of the lily family. They have a subtle flavor that doesn't overpower. The head often has two cloves, each covered with a thin, papery skin. When a recipe calls for one shallot, peel and use as many cloves as you find inside. Shallots are available year round. Store in a cool, dry, well-ventilated place for up to one month.

1 boneless center-cut pork loin roast (about 2 pounds)
2 tablespoons olive oil
1/2 cup diced shallot
2 large cloves garlic, minced
1 package (10 ounces) frozen chopped spinach, thawed and well-drained
1 egg, slightly beaten
1/2 cup Italian seasoned bread crumbs
1 teaspoon dried basil
1 teaspoon Montreal steak seasoning
Kitchen twine
Salt and freshly ground black pepper to taste
Brandy Sauce (recipe on page 88)

Using sharp knife, make horizontal cut 1/2 inch from bottom of roast, cutting to within 1/2 inch of opposite edge. Roll roast exposing cut surface. Continue cutting and rolling to make flat piece of meat. With meat mallet, lightly pound meat to even thickness.

In medium skillet, heat olive oil over medium-high heat. Add shallot and garlic; cook until just tender, about 1 to 2 minutes. Cool slightly. Stir in spinach, egg, bread crumbs, basil and seasoning; spread over cut surface of roast. Roll up jellyroll style toward first cut edge. Tie with kitchen twine to hold together. Season with salt and pepper.

Place roast on rack in shallow roasting pan. Roast in 400° F oven until internal temperature is 155° F, about 1 hour to 1 hour 20 minutes. Cover and let stand 15 minutes before slicing. Serve with Brandy Sauce.

Makes 6-8 servings

Per serving with sauce

Calories 284
Fat 17 g
Cholesterol 88 mg
Sodium 430 mg
Carbohydrate 8 g
Fiber 1 g

Grilled Herb-Rubbed Chops

Brining makes pork chops juicy, and a fresh herb rub adds a burst of flavor. Grill the pork chops quickly over indirect heat to keep them moist.

technique savvy

Brining

Brining ensures tender, juicy poultry and pork. Follow brine recipes exactly for balanced flavors and good texture. Coarse salt (kosher salt) dissolves easily, making it the preferred salt for brines. To substitute table salt, decrease the amount by one-third. Place a saucer or other clean object on top of meat to keep it submerged. Brine in the refrigerator for just the time stated in the recipe. Discard used brine and do not reuse it.

6 bone-in rib chops, about 1-inch thick (about 4 pounds)
2 cloves garlic, minced
1 tablespoon snipped fresh rosemary
1 tablespoon snipped fresh thyme
1 tablespoon chopped fresh parsley
1 tablespoon coarse salt
1 tablespoon freshly ground black pepper

Brine chops according to directions (see recipe).

In small bowl, combine garlic, rosemary, thyme, parsley, salt and pepper. Rub herb mixture onto both sides of chops; let stand for 15 minutes.

Place chops on oiled grid over direct medium-high heat; grill until well browned, about 1 1/2 minutes per side. Move chops to side of grid for indirect heat; cover and grill until internal temperature is 145° F to 150° F, about 5 to 6 minutes per side.

Makes 6 servings

Brine for Chops

3 1/2 cups water
1/4 cup coarse salt
1/4 cup firmly packed brown sugar

Place chops in large freezer-weight reclosable plastic bag; place in deep 6-quart bowl. In 2-quart batter bowl, combine all brine ingredients; stir until salt and sugar dissolve. Pour over chops in bag. Seal bag; refrigerate for 4 to 6 hours. Remove chops from brine; discard brine. Pat dry and cook as directed.

Per serving

Calories 259
Fat 9 g
Cholesterol 94 mg
Sodium 1482 mg
Carbohydrate 2 g
Fiber <1 g

Herb Ginger Pork Medallions

These tender pork medallions are easy enough for a weeknight and special enough for guests. Ginger ale is the surprise ingredient in this flavorful pan sauce.

Step-by-Step Instructions

1 pork tenderloin
  (about 1¼ pounds)
2 teaspoons dried thyme
½ teaspoon salt
½ teaspoon ground black
  pepper
½ teaspoon ground ginger
¼ teaspoon garlic powder
1 tablespoon butter
1 tablespoon cornstarch
1 can (12 ounces) ginger ale
  (divided)

1 Trim and discard fat and silver skin from tenderloin. Cut pork into 1-inch-thick medallions. **2** Flatten slightly with heel of hand. In small bowl, combine thyme, salt, pepper, ginger and garlic powder. Rub spice mixture onto both sides of medallions.

In medium skillet, heat butter over medium-high heat. Add pork; cook until no longer pink, about 4 minutes per side. Transfer meat to platter; cover to keep warm.

In small bowl, dissolve cornstarch in ¼ cup of the ginger ale. Place skillet with drippings over medium heat. Add remaining ginger ale, stirring to scrape browned bits from bottom of pan. Add cornstarch mixture; cook stirring constantly until sauce is thickened, about 2 minutes. Serve sauce over pork.

Makes 4 servings

TIP Silver skin is a thin, translucent membrane that covers pork tenderloin. It is best to remove and discard it before cooking to make the meat more tender and prevent it from curling. Use a sharp knife to loosen the silver skin and gently scrape it away; or grasp it with a paper towel and pull it from the tenderloin.

Per serving

Calories 252
Fat 10 g
Cholesterol 97 mg
Sodium 364 mg
Carbohydrate 11 g
Fiber <1 g

Honey Grilled Tenderloin

You can't beat pork tenderloin for a quick, delicious meal from the grill. This simple honey mustard glaze is one the whole family will love.

2 pork tenderloins
    (about 1¼ pounds each)
2 tablespoons honey
2 tablespoons Dijon-style
    mustard
2 tablespoons soy sauce
2 cloves garlic, minced

Trim fat and silver skin from tenderloins. In small bowl, stir together remaining ingredients.

TO GRILL Place tenderloins on grid over medium-high heat; grill turning and basting frequently with glaze until internal temperature is 155° F, about 25 to 35 minutes. Cover and let stand 10 minutes before slicing.

TO ROAST Place tenderloins on rack in shallow roasting pan. Roast in 350° F oven basting frequently with glaze until internal temperature is 155° F, about 35 minutes. Cover and let stand 10 minutes before slicing.

Makes 8 servings

Per serving

Calories 176
Fat 4 g
Cholesterol 84 mg
Sodium 379 mg
Carbohydrate 5 g
Fiber 0 g

Pork Tenderloin Béarnaise

Simple pan-roasted pork tenderloin topped with our classic Béarnaise Sauce is a recipe you'll turn to again and again. It's a fabulous entrée that's a cinch to prepare.

2 pork tenderloins
    (about 1¼ pounds each)
1 tablespoon vegetable oil
Freshly ground black pepper
    to taste
Béarnaise Sauce (recipe on
    page 90)

Trim fat and silver skin from tenderloins. Brush with oil; sprinkle with freshly ground pepper.

Cook according to directions above, omitting basting with glaze. Cover and let stand 10 minutes before slicing. Serve with Béarnaise Sauce.

Makes 8 servings

Per serving with sauce

Calories 310
Fat 21 g
Cholesterol 176 mg
Sodium 212 mg
Carbohydrate 1 g
Fiber 0 g

Grilled Italian Sausage with Pepper Relish

School of Cooking Manager and sports fan Loretta Evans loves football and good food. Her version of grilled sausage and tangy pepper relish are perfect for a tailgate party or a backyard barbecue.

ingredient savvy

Italian Sausage

A favorite pizza topping and a zesty addition to pasta sauces, Italian sausage is a coarse, fresh pork sausage. Flavored with garlic and fennel seed, Italian sausage may be either sweet and mild or hot, spiked with red pepper. Whether you choose bulk or link sausage, cook it thoroughly until it's no longer pink. Drain it well before adding to recipes.

6 Italian sausage links
1 tablespoon vegetable oil
1 medium red bell pepper, seeded and thinly sliced
1 medium green bell pepper, seeded and thinly sliced
1½ cups thinly sliced onion
1 clove garlic, minced
¼ cup white balsamic vinegar or white wine vinegar
2 teaspoons sugar
2 teaspoons hot pepper sauce
6 hot dog buns

Place sausage links on grid over medium heat; grill turning links often until golden brown and internal temperature is 155° F, about 20 to 25 minutes.

In large skillet over medium-high heat, heat oil. Add peppers, onion and garlic; cover and cook stirring frequently until vegetables are tender, about 5 minutes. Add vinegar, sugar and hot sauce; cook uncovered stirring frequently until liquid evaporates, about 4 to 5 minutes. Serve warm, or cool to room temperature.

Serve sausage on buns with relish.

Makes 6 servings

TIP Pepper Relish can be made 1 day ahead. Cover and refrigerate. Bring to room temperature, or heat in microwave on high for 3 minutes before serving.

Per serving

Calories 437
Fat 25 g
Cholesterol 62 mg
Sodium 717 mg
Carbohydrate 30 g
Fiber 2 g

Glazed Baked Ham

A baked ham topped with a luscious glaze makes a stately centerpiece for a holiday buffet or dinner table.

ingredient savvy

Ham

Fully-cooked ham is a delicious way to serve a crowd. Store a whole ham in its original wrapping in the refrigerator for up to 7 days; a half ham for up to 5 days; and ham slices for 3 to 4 days. Fully-cooked ham may be eaten cold, but heating brings out the savory flavor. Be sure to refrigerate leftovers within 2 hours after serving. Ham may be frozen for 1 to 2 months, but it will not be as moist and tender when thawed.

1 boneless fully-cooked half
    ham (5 to 7 pounds)
Glaze of your choice
    (recipes on page 57)

Remove string net from ham, if necessary. Place in shallow roasting pan just slightly larger than ham. Score ham in diamond pattern. Bake in 325° F oven until internal temperature is 140° F, about 2 hours, basting with glaze during last 30 minutes.

Makes 3-4 servings per pound

BONELESS HAM ROASTING CHART (325° F)	
Half ham (5 to 7 pounds)	18 to 24 minutes per pound
Whole ham (10 to 15 pounds)	15 to 18 minutes per pound
Cook to internal temperature of 140° F	

Per 3-ounce serving

Calories 184
Fat 10 g
Cholesterol 60 mg
Sodium 1449 mg
Carbohydrate 3 g
Fiber 0 g

Sweetly Spiced Ham Glaze

½ cup pineapple preserves
¼ cup firmly packed brown
    sugar
2 teaspoons Dijon-style
    mustard
½ teaspoon ground
    cinnamon
½ teaspoon hot pepper
    sauce

In small bowl, stir together all ingredients. Brush glaze over ham during last 30 minutes of baking.

Makes ¾ cup

Per 2 tablespoons

Calories 99
Fat 0 g
Cholesterol 0 mg
Sodium 68 mg
Carbohydrate 25 g
Fiber <1 g

Cranberry Ham Glaze

⅓ cup cranapple juice
    cocktail concentrate,
    undiluted
⅓ cup pure maple syrup

In small bowl, stir together juice concentrate and syrup. Brush glaze over ham during last 30 minutes of baking.

Makes ⅔ cup

Per 2 tablespoons

Calories 87
Fat 0 g
Cholesterol 0 mg
Sodium 2 mg
Carbohydrate 25 g
Fiber 0 g

Praline Ham Glaze

¾ cup firmly packed brown
    sugar
¼ cup honey
2 tablespoons butter
½ cup finely chopped
    pecans

In 1-quart glass measure, combine brown sugar, honey and butter. Microwave (high) stirring occasionally until mixture boils, about 2 to 3 minutes. Stir in pecans. Spoon glaze over ham during last 30 minutes of baking.

Makes ¾ cup

Per 2 tablespoons

Calories 244
Fat 11 g
Cholesterol 11 mg
Sodium 12 mg
Carbohydrate 40 g
Fiber 1 g

Jalapeño Lime Shrimp with Roasted Garlic Couscous
Recipe on page 60

Jalapeño Lime Shrimp with Roasted Garlic Couscous

Season quick-cooking couscous with roasted garlic, then top it with spicy grilled shrimp for a lively change-of-pace entrée.

ingredient savvy

Couscous

These tiny pearls of pasta are at the heart of North African cuisine, but are right at home in all sorts of dishes. Look for boxes of couscous (KOOS-koos) in the rice and pasta section. Couscous cooks very quickly so it's perfect for easy weeknight meals. Add extra flavor by cooking couscous in chicken broth instead of water, or stirring in your favorite seasonings. Serve it as you would pasta or rice as a complement to grilled meats or hearty stews.

1 1/2 pounds extra-large (26 to 30 count) shrimp, peeled and deveined
1/2 cup fresh lime juice
1/2 cup fresh orange juice
1/4 cup honey
2 jalapeño peppers, seeded and finely chopped, OR
   1/4 cup prepared chopped jalapeño peppers
3 cloves garlic, minced
1 teaspoon ground cumin
1/4 teaspoon salt
3 cloves garlic, slivered
1 tablespoon olive oil
2 cups water
1 box (10 ounces) couscous

Place shrimp in large reclosable plastic bag. In 2-cup glass measure, combine lime juice, orange juice, honey, jalapeños, the minced garlic, cumin and salt. Pour 3/4 cup of the marinade into bag with shrimp; reserve remaining 1/2 cup marinade for couscous. Seal bag and turn to coat shrimp. Place bag on plate and marinate in refrigerator for 30 minutes.

Place the slivered garlic on sheet of heavy-duty foil. Drizzle olive oil over garlic. Fold foil into tightly sealed packet. Place foil packet on grid over medium-high heat; grill turning occasionally until packet puffs slightly, about 10 minutes.

Soak wooden skewers in water for 10 minutes. Thread shrimp in "C" shape onto skewers. Place skewers on oiled grid over medium-high heat; grill until shrimp are opaque, about 3 minutes per side.

In medium saucepan, bring water and reserved marinade just to boiling over high heat. Remove from heat. Stir in couscous and roasted garlic slivers. Cover and let stand 5 minutes. Fluff couscous with fork and arrange on serving plates. Top with skewers of shrimp.

Makes 4 servings

Per serving

Calories 508
Fat 7 g
Cholesterol 259 mg
Sodium 280 mg
Carbohydrate 65 g
Fiber 4 g

Photograph on page 58

Champagne Shrimp Risotto

Look no further for that special-occasion entrée. Creamy risotto with tender shrimp and a splash of Champagne will impress even the most discriminating dinner guest.

1 can (14 ounces) chicken
   broth
1 cup Champagne or
   dry white wine
½ cup water
2 tablespoons butter
1 cup arborio rice
¼ cup finely chopped
   shallots
1 pound large (43 to
   50 count) shrimp, peeled
   and deveined
¼ cup finely chopped red
   bell pepper
1 teaspoon chopped fresh
   rosemary
⅓ cup grated parmesan
   cheese
Freshly ground black
   pepper

In medium saucepan, heat broth, Champagne and water over medium heat until hot, but not boiling.

In large saucepan, melt butter over medium heat. Add rice and shallots; cook stirring constantly for 1 minute. Add 1 cup hot broth mixture; cook stirring often until broth is absorbed. Add remaining broth mixture, 1 cup at a time, cooking and stirring often until liquid is absorbed before adding additional broth.

When rice is tender and creamy, stir in shrimp, bell pepper and rosemary. Cook stirring often until shrimp are opaque, about 3 to 5 minutes. Stir in cheese. Season with pepper.

Makes 4 servings

ingredient savvy

Champagne

While many sparkling wines from around the world are referred to as "Champagne," the real thing is made in the region of northeast France that bears the same name. Check the label to determine the level of sweetness; *brut* is the driest; *extra sec* or *extra dry* is slightly sweeter; *sec* is medium sweet; and *demi-sec* is very sweet. Italy's *spumante* and Germany's *sekt* are on the sweeter end of the spectrum.

Per serving

Calories 418
Fat 10 g
Cholesterol 195 mg
Sodium 709 mg
Carbohydrate 42 g
Fiber 1 g

Creamy Eggs with Chipotle Crab Hollandaise

Guests will love this elegant brunch dish with a little attitude. Rich hollandaise sauce spiked with crab and chipotle chiles makes a lively topping for creamy scrambled eggs.

ingredient savvy

Chipotles in Adobo Sauce

Chipotles (chih-POHT-lays) – those little hot peppers with wrinkled, dark red skin – are actually smoked jalapeños. They are generally canned in adobo sauce, a piquant blend of tomatoes and spices. Because just a little bit of pepper adds a big burst of flavor, purée the chiles with the sauce and freeze the purée in a freezer-weight plastic bag. Break off a piece as needed to add a touch of smoky heat to mayonnaise, dips, chili – all sorts of dishes.

No-Fail Hollandaise Sauce (recipe on page 90), OR 1 package (1.25 ounces) hollandaise sauce mix, prepared according to package directions
1 can (6.5 ounces) white crab meat, drained and flaked
2 to 3 teaspoons puréed chipotle chiles in adobo sauce
12 large eggs
1 teaspoon salt
$1/2$ teaspoon ground white pepper
2 tablespoons butter
4 ounces ($1/2$ of 8-ounce package) cream cheese, cubed and softened
2 tablespoons snipped fresh chives
6 English muffins, split and toasted, OR 6 frozen puff pastry shells, baked according to package directions

Prepare Hollandaise Sauce. Stir in crab and chipotle purée. Set aside and keep warm.

In large bowl, whisk eggs with salt and pepper. In large skillet, melt butter over medium heat. Add eggs; cook and stir until almost set, about 1 minute. Add cream cheese and chives; cook and stir until cheese melts and eggs are softly set, about 2 minutes.

Divide eggs evenly among English muffins. Top with Chipotle Crab Hollandaise.

Makes 6 servings

Per serving

Calories 485
Fat 33 g
Cholesterol 547 mg
Sodium 1107 mg
Carbohydrate 28 g
Fiber 2 g

Overnight Crab Manicotti

Elegance meets ease in this make-ahead recipe that's great for entertaining. Fill the uncooked noodles and refrigerate in the sauce overnight, and it's ready to bake the next day.

1 jar (16 ounces) Alfredo sauce
1 cup milk
1 carton (15 ounces) ricotta cheese
1 package (10 ounces) frozen chopped spinach, thawed and undrained
1 can (6.5 ounces) white crab meat, undrained
8 ounces (2 cups) shredded Italian cheese blend (divided)
3 cloves garlic, minced
1 box (8 ounces) manicotti noodles
½ cup Italian seasoned bread crumbs or fresh bread crumbs

In medium bowl, combine Alfredo sauce and milk; spread thin layer in 9x13-inch baking dish that has been coated with no-stick cooking spray.

In medium bowl, combine ¼ cup of the Alfredo sauce mixture, ricotta cheese, spinach, crab meat, 1 cup of the shredded cheese and garlic; stir until blended. Place mixture in large freezer-weight reclosable plastic bag; seal bag and cut off one corner. Pipe filling into uncooked noodles. Arrange filled noodles in baking dish. Pipe any remaining filling between noodles.

Cover noodles with remaining sauce; sprinkle remaining 1 cup shredded cheese over top. Cover with foil and refrigerate overnight.

Bake covered in 350° F oven for 45 minutes. Uncover; sprinkle bread crumbs over top and bake until lightly browned and sauce is bubbly, about 10 minutes.

Makes 6 servings

ingredient savvy

Canned Crab

Enjoy your favorite crab dishes anytime at a price that's right for you. Jumbo crab meat is the most elegant, with large succulent pieces and a delicate flavor. Backfin lump is a good choice for most dishes. White crab meat is ideal for crab cakes and salads. Claw crab meat is a great value and has a more robust flavor that stands up to spicy seasonings. Imitation crab meat, also called surimi, is actually Alaska pollock – a mild white fish – that's colored, flavored and formed to look like crab.

Per serving

Calories 591
Fat 32 g
Cholesterol 123 mg
Sodium 1291 mg
Carbohydrate 48 g
Fiber 2 g

Seared Scallops with Maple Ginger Cream

Tender pan-seared scallops get dressed for dinner in a silky cream sauce flavored with a drizzle of maple syrup and a hint of ginger.

ingredient savvy

Scallops

Sweet, succulent scallops are a seafood lover's delight! Bay scallops, usually found off the East Coast, are tiny and number about 100 per pound. Sea scallops are larger and average about 30 per pound. Whether large or small, cook scallops quickly – just until they're opaque – so they stay delicate, tender and buttery.

1½ pounds sea scallops, thawed if frozen
2 tablespoons butter
2 carrots, cut into matchstick-size pieces
1 teaspoon grated fresh ginger root
1 cup heavy whipping cream
2 tablespoons pure maple syrup
2 teaspoons Dijon-style mustard
Salt and ground white pepper to taste
12 ounces angel hair pasta, cooked according to package directions
2 tablespoons snipped fresh chives

Rinse and drain scallops; pat dry. In large skillet, melt butter over medium-high heat. Add carrots and ginger; cover and cook until carrots are crisp-tender, about 2 minutes. Remove carrots from skillet; set aside.

Working in batches, add scallops to skillet; cook until opaque, about 2 minutes per side. Transfer scallops to plate with carrots; cover to keep warm while cooking remaining scallops.

Add cream, maple syrup and mustard to skillet; bring to a boil. Reduce heat and simmer until slightly thickened, about 3 to 4 minutes. Add scallops, carrots, salt and pepper; cook for 1 minute. Spoon scallop mixture over hot cooked pasta. Garnish with snipped chives.

Makes 6 servings

Per serving

Calories 510
Fat 21 g
Cholesterol 102 mg
Sodium 280 mg
Carbohydrate 53 g
Fiber 2 g

Angel Hair Pasta with White Clam Sauce

technique savvy

Steaming Fresh Clams

Fresh clams steamed in their shells are a special treat. Purchase clams with unbroken, tightly closed shells. Keep them refrigerated and cook them within 1 to 2 days. Tap any that are slightly opened and discard any that don't quickly snap shut. Soak clams for 1 hour in a solution of 1 gallon cold water plus 1/3 cup salt to remove sand, discarding any clams that float. Place clams in a steamer basket over simmering water. Cook just until the shells open, about 3 to 4 minutes.

School of Cooking instructor Carolyn Pokorny is known for her creative presentation ideas and, of course, her delicious recipes. This delicate pasta with a light sauce, compliments of Carolyn, is no exception.

2 cans (6.5 ounces each) chopped clams, drained, reserving liquid
1 bottle (8 ounces) clam juice
1/2 cup low-sodium chicken broth
1/2 cup heavy whipping cream (not 40% gourmet cream)
3 tablespoons butter
2 large cloves garlic, minced
3 1/2 tablespoons flour
3 tablespoons minced fresh parsley
2 1/2 teaspoons dried basil, crushed
2/3 cup grated parmesan cheese (divided)
Salt and freshly ground black pepper to taste
12 to 16 ounces angel hair pasta, cooked according to package directions
Fresh basil sprigs for garnish (optional)
4 to 6 fresh clams, steamed, for garnish (optional)

In 4-cup glass measure, combine reserved liquid from canned clams, bottled clam juice, chicken broth and cream. Microwave (high) for 1 to 2 minutes; set aside.

In medium skillet, melt butter over medium heat. Add garlic; cook until soft, about 1 minute. Stir in flour; cook stirring constantly for 1 minute. Add heated clam juice mixture, parsley and dried basil; cook until thickened and hot, about 2 to 3 minutes. Add 1/3 cup of the parmesan cheese; cook until cheese is melted. Season with salt and pepper. Add drained clams; cook just until hot, about 1 to 2 minutes. (Over-cooking will toughen clams.)

Place pasta on serving plates. Top with hot clam sauce and remaining parmesan cheese. If desired, garnish with fresh basil and steamed clams.

Makes 4-6 servings

Per serving

Calories 403
Fat 17 g
Cholesterol 52 mg
Sodium 502 mg
Carbohydrate 47 g
Fiber 2 g

Smoked Salmon with Chutney Sauce

Hickory chips give grilled salmon a sweet, smoky flavor. The tangy, chutney-flavored mayonnaise is a terrific accompaniment.

1 salmon fillet
  (about 2 1/2 pounds)
2 teaspoons cracked black
  pepper
4 cups hickory chips, soaked
  in water
1 cup mayonnaise
1/2 cup mango chutney
1 clove garlic, minced

Season salmon with pepper. Add 2 cups of the chips to medium-hot coals. Push coals to one side of grill. Place salmon flesh-side down on oiled grid over indirect heat; cover and grill for 15 minutes. Turn fish skin-side down with large metal spatula. Add remaining 2 cups chips; cover and grill until salmon is just opaque throughout and internal temperature is 145° F, about 15 minutes. Slide spatula between skin and flesh; remove from grill. Discard skin. In small bowl, stir together remaining ingredients. Serve salmon with sauce.

Makes 8-10 servings

TIP For easy cleanup, see Chai Glazed Salmon Tip (page 69).

Per serving

Calories 416
Fat 30 g
Cholesterol 74 mg
Sodium 331 mg
Carbohydrate 12 g
Fiber <1 g

Teriyaki Grilled Salmon

The classic sweet and salty flavors of teriyaki are a great fit with the rich flavor of salmon. It's an easy entrée from the grill that the whole family will love.

1 salmon fillet
  (about 1 1/2 pounds)
1 tablespoon brown sugar
1 tablespoon soy sauce
1 tablespoon dry sherry
1 tablespoon grated fresh
  ginger root
2 to 3 cloves garlic, minced
1/4 cup thinly sliced green
  onion

Cut salmon into 4 to 6 equal portions, cutting to, but not through skin. In small bowl, stir together brown sugar, soy sauce, sherry, ginger and garlic. Place salmon flesh-side down on oiled grid over medium-high heat; cover and grill for 4 minutes. Turn fish skin-side down with large metal spatula. Spoon ginger mixture over salmon; cover and grill until just opaque throughout and internal temperature is 145° F, about 10 minutes per inch of thickness. Slide spatula between skin and flesh; remove from grill. Discard skin. Garnish with green onion.

Makes 4-6 servings

TIP For easy cleanup, see Chai Glazed Salmon Tip (page 69).

Per serving

Calories 224
Fat 12 g
Cholesterol 66 mg
Sodium 222 mg
Carbohydrate 3 g
Fiber <1 g

Chai Glazed Salmon

Aromatic tea makes a basting sauce that is perfect with flavorful salmon. Grill vegetables of your choice alongside the salmon, basting frequently with the tea glaze.

2 black chai tea bags
½ cup boiling water
2 tablespoons snipped fresh chives
1 clove garlic, minced
2 tablespoons olive oil
2 tablespoons honey
1 tablespoon soy sauce
2 teaspoons minced fresh ginger root
¼ teaspoon salt
¼ teaspoon crushed red pepper flakes
1 salmon fillet (about 1½ to 2 pounds), cut into 6 strips

Place tea bags in 1-cup glass measure; pour boiling water over tea bags. Steep for 5 minutes; discard tea bags. Stir in remaining ingredients except salmon. Cover and let stand for 30 minutes or refrigerate overnight.

TO GRILL Place salmon flesh-side down on oiled grid over medium-high heat; cover and grill for 4 minutes. Turn fish skin-side down with large metal spatula. Stir glaze and spoon over fish; cover and grill, occasionally spooning additional glaze over salmon until opaque throughout and internal temperature is 145° F, about 10 minutes per inch of thickness. Slide spatula between skin and flesh; remove from grill. Discard skin.

TO BROIL Place salmon flesh-side up on rack of broiler pan that has been lightly coated with no-stick cooking spray. Stir glaze and spoon over fish. Broil 6 inches from heat source, occasionally spooning additional glaze over salmon until opaque throughout and internal temperature is 145° F, about 10 minutes per inch of thickness.

Makes 6 servings

TIP For easy cleanup and serving, place sheet of heavy-duty foil on grid alongside salmon while it grills flesh-side down. Turn fish and place skin-side down on top of preheated foil. When salmon is done, slide metal spatula between flesh and skin. Skin will stick to foil. Discard foil.

ingredient savvy

Chai Tea

Chai is a spicy tea blend that originated in India. It is flavored with pungent spices like cardamom, cinnamon, cloves – even black pepper. Chai is brewed strong and served steaming hot or ice cold with milk and sugar. Using tea as an ingredient in recipes adds depth and richness to the dish.

Per serving

Calories 213
Fat 13 g
Cholesterol 66 mg
Sodium 92 mg
Carbohydrate 1 g
Fiber 0 g

Lemony Grilled Fish Steaks

Before Dierbergs prints a recipe for consumers, it gets final-tested and tasted by Test Kitchen Manager Karen Hurych. This recipe is one of her favorites for a quick and delicious dinner.

technique savvy

Is It Done?

Whether you're in the mood to broil, bake, sauté or grill, it's easy to have perfectly cooked fish every time. Arrange fish in a baking dish or broiler pan and tuck under any thin ends so the fillets are a uniform thickness. Measure fish at its thickest spot, then cook it 10 minutes per inch of thickness. Fish is done when the flesh is opaque and the internal temperature reaches 145° F. Mild white fish varieties will also flake easily with a fork.

1 to 1¼ pounds fish steaks (tuna, salmon or swordfish)
Salt and freshly ground black pepper to taste
2 tablespoons chopped fresh parsley
1 tablespoon olive oil
1 teaspoon grated lemon peel
1 tablespoon fresh lemon juice
1 clove garlic, minced

Season fish steaks with salt and pepper. In small bowl, stir together remaining ingredients.

TO GRILL Place fish on oiled grid over medium-high heat; brush generously with lemon mixture. Cover and grill, brushing occasionally with lemon mixture until fish is opaque throughout and internal temperature is 145° F, about 4 to 5 minutes per side.

TO BROIL Place steaks on rack of broiler pan that has been lightly coated with no-stick cooking spray; brush generously with lemon mixture. Broil 6 inches from heat source, brushing occasionally with lemon mixture until fish is opaque throughout and internal temperature is 145° F, about 10 minutes per inch of thickness.

Makes 4 servings

Per serving

Calories 154
Fat 4 g
Cholesterol 51 mg
Sodium 43 mg
Carbohydrate 1 g
Fiber <1 g

Shrimp

No matter how you prepare them, freshly cooked shrimp are a special treat. Shrimp cook quickly and are done when they turn pink and are opaque throughout. Don't overcook or they become tough.

ingredient savvy

Shrimp
(sold by size or count)

Size	Number per pound
Jumbo	16 to 20 per pound
Extra-large	26 to 30 per pound
Large	43 to 50 per pound

Whole Lobster

Size	Cooking Time
1 to 1¼ pounds	10 to 12 minutes
1½ to 2 pounds	15 to 18 minutes
2½ to 5 pounds	20 to 25 minutes

Larger shrimp are more expensive, but make a more impressive presentation and take less time to clean.

Cooking shrimp in the shell gives the best flavor and texture. To devein shrimp in the shell, use kitchen shears to cut along the back edge of the shell. Remove the vein under cold running water.

TO BOIL Bring water to a boil in large saucepan. Add deveined shrimp and spices, if desired. Cover, remove pan from heat, and let stand until shrimp are pink and opaque, about 5 to 6 minutes. Serve hot or chilled.

TO MICROWAVE Arrange ½ pound deveined shrimp in the shell around inside edge of glass pie plate, with tails to the center. Cover loosely. Microwave (high) for 1½ to 2 minutes or until shrimp are opaque. Cool slightly; peel if desired.

TO GRILL Place 1 pound deveined shrimp in single layer on sheet of heavy-duty foil; drizzle 1 tablespoon olive oil and sprinkle 1 teaspoon Cajun/Creole seasoning over shrimp. Fold foil to form tightly sealed packet. Place packet on grid over medium-high heat; grill until packet is puffed, about 5 minutes. Let stand 1 to 2 minutes before opening. Shrimp should be pink and opaque throughout.

TO GRILL ON SKEWERS Soak wooden skewers in cold water for at least 10 minutes to prevent charring during cooking. Peel and devein shrimp, leaving tails intact. Thread shrimp in "C" shape onto each skewer. Place skewers on oiled grid over medium-high heat; grill until shrimp are opaque, about 2 to 3 minutes per side.

King Crab Legs

Melted butter with a squeeze of fresh lemon juice is the perfect dipping sauce for sweet, succulent crab legs.

TO BROIL Partially thaw crab for 2 to 3 hours in refrigerator. Split legs lengthwise. Place on baking sheet. Brush with melted butter. Broil 4 to 6 inches from heat source until crab legs turn red, about 4 to 5 minutes. Serve with clarified butter.

TO STEAM Pour 1 inch water into large saucepan; place steamer basket over water. Place frozen crab legs in steamer basket. Bring water to a boil; cover and steam for 8 to 10 minutes. Serve with clarified butter.

Frozen Lobster Tail

Easy to prepare and serve, lobster tail is a simple, yet elegant entrée.

For food safety, thaw lobster tail in the refrigerator for 24 hours.

TO STEAM Pour 1 inch water into large saucepan; place steamer basket over water. Bring water to a boil. Place tails in their shells in steamer basket; cover and steam until shells are reddish in color and the meat firm and opaque, about 10 to 12 minutes. Serve with clarified butter.

TO GRILL Steam tails as directed. Remove meat from shell; brush with melted butter. Place tails on grid over direct medium heat. Grill until lightly browned, about 1 to 2 minutes per side. Serve with clarified butter.

TO BROIL Steam tails as directed. Remove meat from shell; brush with melted butter. Place tails on rack of broiler pan; dust with paprika. Broil 4 to 6 inches from heat source until lightly browned, about 1 to 2 minutes per side (do not overcook). Serve with clarified butter.

TO SERVE Place tail on its back. Using kitchen shears, cut down center through shell and membrane. Split open shell; remove cooked meat.

Fresh Whole Lobster

Sweet, succulent lobster is nothing less than luxurious. Dip every delicious bite in clarified butter.

For food safety, purchase lobster no more than 24 hours before serving; store in refrigerator. Keep lobster alive until the moment it is cooked.

TO BOIL In 10- to 12-quart pot, heat water to a rapid boil. Submerge live lobster head first into water. Cover immediately. Return water to a boil; reduce heat and simmer. When cooked, lobster shell will be reddish in color and meat will be firm and opaque. Serve with clarified butter.

technique savvy

Clarified Butter

In small saucepan, melt 1 cup butter (2 sticks) over low heat until 3 layers form; remove from heat. Skim off top layer of white foam with spoon. Let butter sit until milk solids settle on bottom, about 5 minutes. Strain mixture through coffee filter or fine sieve; discard filter. Place clarified butter in covered container and store in refrigerator for up to 6 months.

MEATLESS
entrées

Campanelle with Asparagus and Pine Nuts
Recipe on page 76

Campanelle with Asparagus and Pine Nuts

Light, fresh and colorful, this pasta showcases asparagus at its best. Crunchy pine nuts add an authentic Italian touch.

ingredient savvy

Pine Nuts

Pine nuts – also called *piñon* or *pignoli* – are found inside certain varieties of pine cones. Extracting them is a very tedious process, which makes them more expensive than other nuts. Pine nuts have a high fat content and turn rancid quickly, so store them in the refrigerator for up to 3 months or freeze them for up to 9 months. Pine nuts are most frequently used in Italian pesto, but add a nutty crunch to salads and other dishes.

1 pound asparagus, trimmed and cut into bite-sized pieces (about 3 cups)
4 cloves garlic, minced
2 teaspoons olive oil
1 can (14 ounces) chicken broth
2 tablespoons fresh lemon juice
1 tablespoon cornstarch
1/2 cup roasted red bell peppers, drained and sliced
1/2 cup pine nuts, toasted
1/2 cup fresh basil, cut into strips
Salt and pepper to taste
1 box (16 ounces) campanelle pasta or other medium pasta, cooked according to package directions

In large skillet over medium-high heat, cook asparagus and garlic in olive oil until crisp-tender, about 3 minutes.

In 2-cup glass measure, combine broth, lemon juice and cornstarch; stir until cornstarch dissolves. Stir into vegetables. Cook stirring frequently until slightly thickened, about 1 to 2 minutes. Gently stir in roasted peppers, pine nuts, basil, salt and pepper. Toss with hot cooked pasta.

Makes 8 servings

Per serving

Calories 300
Fat 8 g
Cholesterol 1 mg
Sodium 219 mg
Carbohydrate 48 g
Fiber 3 g

Photograph on page 74

Baked Penne with Mozzarella

There's no need to cook the pasta ahead. Simply stir everything together and bake for a satisfying one-dish dinner.

1 jar (7 ounces) roasted red bell peppers, drained
1 jar (26 ounces) spaghetti sauce
1 cup chicken broth
8 ounces penne pasta
1 cup sliced mushrooms
1 can (2.25 ounces) sliced ripe or kalamata olives, drained
2 cloves garlic, minced
1 teaspoon dried basil
1 teaspoon dried oregano
4 ounces mozzarella cheese

Cut roasted peppers into 1-inch pieces; place in large bowl. Add remaining ingredients except mozzarella cheese; stir to combine. Place in 9x13-inch baking dish that has been coated with no-stick cooking spray. Cover and bake in 350° F oven for 1 hour stirring halfway through baking time. Cut cheese into ½-inch cubes; stir into pasta and serve immediately.

Makes 6-8 servings

Per serving

Calories 233
Fat 8 g
Cholesterol 9 mg
Sodium 1044 mg
Carbohydrate 34 g
Fiber 2 g

Greek Vegetable Pasta

This colorful and hearty dish is ready in just minutes. Toss rigatoni with a harvest of vegetables for a dish brimming with sunny Mediterranean flavors.

2 tablespoons olive oil
1 medium onion, chopped
2 cloves garlic, minced
2 cans (14 to 16 ounces each) stewed tomatoes, undrained
1 small eggplant, peeled and cubed
1 small yellow squash, cubed
1 small zucchini, cubed
2 teaspoons dried oregano, crushed
1½ teaspoons lemon pepper seasoning
1 can (2.25 ounces) sliced ripe or kalamata olives, drained
Hot cooked rigatoni or mostaccioli
1 package (4 ounces) reduced-fat feta cheese, crumbled

In large nonstick skillet, heat olive oil over medium-high heat. Add onion and garlic; cook stirring occasionally until onion is tender, about 5 minutes. Add stewed tomatoes, eggplant, squash, zucchini, oregano and lemon pepper. Reduce heat, cover and simmer until vegetables are tender, about 5 minutes. Stir in olives. Serve over hot cooked pasta; sprinkle cheese over top.

Makes 4-6 servings

Per serving

Calories 315
Fat 10 g
Cholesterol 6 mg
Sodium 722 mg
Carbohydrate 49 g
Fiber 6 g

Portabella Panini

Italy's version of a great grilled sandwich is called panini. This crisp, golden sandwich filled with savory mushrooms and melting cheese is perfect for an easy supper for two.

2 portabella mushrooms
(about 1½ pounds)
6 tablespoons butter,
softened (divided)
4 slices artisan bread
(about ½-inch thick)
4 slices provolone or fontina
cheese
¼ cup baby spinach leaves

Rinse mushrooms; pat dry. Remove and discard stems.
1 Use spoon to scrape dark gills from underside of caps. Slice caps ¼-inch thick. In large skillet, melt 2 tablespoons of the butter over medium-high heat. Add mushrooms; cover and cook until mushrooms are softened, about 5 minutes. Uncover and cook until tender and most of the liquid has evaporated, about 2 minutes. Remove from heat.

Place one slice of cheese on two slices of bread. Top with spinach leaves, mushrooms and remaining cheese and bread. Spread 1 tablespoon of the butter on top side of each sandwich. **2** Place sandwiches buttered-side down in grill pan over medium heat; place foil-wrapped brick or heavy pan on top to compress sandwiches. Cook until golden brown, about 3 minutes.

Spread butter over tops of sandwiches; turn and place brick on sandwiches. Cook until golden brown, about 3 minutes. Serve immediately.

Makes 2 servings

TIP For dynamite flavor, use Dierbergs Cabernet Grille Butter instead of plain butter.

Step-by-step Instructions

Per serving

Calories 884
Fat 52 g
Cholesterol 131 mg
Sodium 1412 mg
Carbohydrate 69 g
Fiber 12 g

Veggie Pizza with Fennel and Smoked Mozzarella

Staff Home Economist Pam Pahl loves mixing lots of colors, flavors and textures into her meatless menus. This terrific pizza delivers all three for a delicious change of pace.

ingredient savvy

Fresh Fennel

Sometimes labeled as *anise*, this aromatic plant has a bulbous base with long, celery-like stems and feathery leaves that look like fresh dill. The base and stems may be eaten fresh in salads, or baked, braised or added to soups. Fresh fennel has a mild, sweet flavor with just a faint hint of licorice that becomes even more delicate when cooked. For extra flavor, snip the feathery leaves and use as a last-minute seasoning.

CRUST
2 cups flour
1/2 teaspoon salt
1 envelope (2 1/4 teaspoons) fast-rising dry yeast
2/3 cup warm (110° to 115° F) water
2 tablespoons vegetable oil

TOPPING
1/2 cup sun-dried tomato pesto
1/2 cup drained and quartered artichoke hearts
1/2 cup sliced fresh fennel
1/2 cup sliced red onion
1/2 cup sliced cremini mushrooms
1 can (2.25 ounces) sliced ripe olives, drained
1/4 cup roasted red bell pepper, drained and sliced
4 ounces smoked mozzarella cheese, shredded (about 1 cup), or 1 cup shredded mozzarella cheese
3/4 cup shredded fresh basil leaves

FOR CRUST Place flour and salt in work bowl of food processor fitted with steel knife blade. In 1-cup glass measure, dissolve yeast in warm water; add oil. With machine running, pour liquid mixture through feed tube in slow, steady stream; process until dough forms a ball and cleans sides of bowl.

Turn out dough onto floured surface and knead several times. Roll and press dough to cover bottom of floured 12-inch pizza pan. Bake in 400° F oven until lightly browned, about 8 minutes.

FOR TOPPING Layer topping ingredients except fresh basil onto partially baked crust in order listed. Bake until crust is lightly browned on bottom and cheese is melted and bubbly, about 8 to 10 minutes. Sprinkle basil over pizza.

Makes 4-6 servings

Per serving

Calories 339
Fat 16 g
Cholesterol 10 mg
Sodium 672 mg
Carbohydrate 41 g
Fiber 2 g

Vegetable Wellingtons

Flaky puff pastry is filled with hearty vegetables and rich gouda cheese for a special entrée. A drizzle of Marsala Sauce adds an elegant touch.

t e c h i n q u e   s a v v y

Using Puff Pastry

Frozen puff pastry equals easy elegance in a box! For crisp pastry, bake it at a high temperature on a parchment-lined baking sheet. Add color and shine to the pastry by brushing it with a mixture of 1 egg beaten with 1 tablespoon water before baking. Use the egg mixture to seal edges, or to attach pastry cutouts to the top for a decorative touch.

½ cup thinly sliced red bell pepper
½ cup chopped shallots
1 tablespoon olive oil
1 cup sliced mushrooms
1 bunch broccolini, coarsely chopped
½ teaspoon herbes de Provence
1 sheet (½ of 17.3-ounce box) frozen puff pastry, thawed
2 ounces smoked gouda cheese, shredded (about ½ cup)
1 egg, beaten with 1 tablespoon water
Marsala Sauce (recipe on page 89)

In medium skillet, cook bell pepper and shallots in olive oil over medium-high heat for 3 minutes. Add mushrooms, broccolini and herbes de Provence. Cook until crisp-tender, about 3 minutes. Cool completely.

On lightly floured surface, roll pastry sheet into 12-inch square. Cut into four 6-inch squares. Place 2 tablespoons cheese and ½ cup vegetable mixture on each square. Brush edges with egg mixture; fold corners of pastry to center, pressing to seal well. Place seam-side down on parchment-lined jellyroll pan. Brush top and sides of pastry with egg mixture.

Bake in 400° F oven until golden brown, about 15 to 20 minutes. Serve with Marsala Sauce.

Makes 4 servings

Per serving

Calories 410
Fat 26 g
Cholesterol 69 mg
Sodium 650 mg
Carbohydrate 29 g
Fiber 1 g

Fresh Asparagus Frittata

Filled with tender asparagus and creamy pepper-jack cheese, this open-faced omelet is ready in minutes. It's great for a quick brunch or dinner.

½ pound asparagus,
  trimmed and cut into
  bite-sized pieces
  (about 1½ cups)
1 tablespoon olive oil
8 eggs
½ cup milk
1½ teaspoons dried basil
¼ teaspoon salt
4 ounces pepper-jack
  cheese, shredded
  (about 1 cup)

In large ovenproof skillet, cook asparagus in olive oil over medium heat until tender, about 3 to 4 minutes.

In medium bowl, whisk together eggs, milk, basil and salt. Pour into skillet over asparagus; cook until edges begin to set. Cook gently, lifting egg mixture from bottom of skillet with spatula so uncooked egg mixture flows to bottom of skillet, about 4 to 5 minutes.

When eggs are still very moist, sprinkle cheese over top. Broil until cheese is slightly brown, about 2 minutes. Serve immediately.

Makes 6 servings

TIP If skillet handle is not ovenproof, wrap it in a double layer of heavy-duty foil to protect it during broiling.

cuisine savvy

Frittata

The Italian cousin of the French omelet, a frittata usually has its ingredients stirred into the eggs rather than folded inside. The egg mixture is cooked slowly over low heat, giving a frittata a firmer texture than an omelet. Topped with cheese and finished under the broiler, it's a delicious meal-in-one for breakfast, brunch or a quick weeknight supper.

Per serving

Calories 210
Fat 15 g
Cholesterol 304 mg
Sodium 326 mg
Carbohydrate 4 g
Fiber 1 g

Classic Quiche Lorraine

As a student living in France, School of Cooking instructor Denise Hall learned to prepare many French dishes. This rich, creamy quiche is a classic.

c u i s i n e   s a v v y

Quiche

This classic egg dish is named for the Alsace-Lorraine region of northeastern France where it began. Quiche is a creamy egg custard typically flavored with herbs and cheese and baked in a pastry shell. All sorts of variations abound using ham, shellfish or vegetables. Quiche Lorraine features crisp bacon and gruyère cheese. With or without meat, quiche makes a delicious brunch, lunch or dinner entrée.

1½ cups flour
6 tablespoons butter, chilled and cut into small cubes
2 tablespoons solid shortening, chilled and cut into small cubes
½ teaspoon salt
Pinch sugar
4½ tablespoons cold water
6 to 8 slices lean bacon (medium thickness), diced and cooked crisp, OR 4 ounces diced cooked ham, sautéed in butter (optional)
3 eggs
1½ cups heavy whipping cream or half-and-half
½ teaspoon salt
Pinch ground black pepper
Pinch ground nutmeg
4 ounces gruyère, fontina or swiss cheese, shredded (about 1 cup)

In work bowl of food processor fitted with steel knife blade, combine flour, butter, shortening, salt and sugar; process until particles resemble coarse crumbs, about 15 seconds. With machine running, pour water all at once through feed tube; process until dough forms a ball.

Butter inside of straight-sided 9-inch tart pan with removable bottom. Press dough lightly into bottom and up sides of pan. Trim off excess dough. Pierce bottom of pastry with fork at ½-inch intervals. Firmly press buttered foil or parchment paper into bottom and up sides of pastry. Fill with dried beans or pie weights.

Place tart pan on jellyroll pan. Bake in 400° F oven until pastry is set, about 8 to 9 minutes. Remove foil and beans. Pierce bottom of pastry with fork. Bake until pastry begins to brown and shrink from sides of pan, about 2 to 3 minutes. Reduce oven temperature to 375° F.

If desired, sprinkle bacon over partially cooked pastry shell. In large mixing bowl, whisk together eggs, cream and seasonings until well blended; stir in cheese. Pour mixture into pastry shell. Bake in upper third of 375° F oven until lightly browned on top and knife inserted in center comes out clean, about 25 to 30 minutes.

Makes 6 servings

Per serving

Calories 581
Fat 48 g
Cholesterol 240 mg
Sodium 511 mg
Carbohydrate 26 g
Fiber 1 g

Overnight Brunch Casserole

Get a head start on a good morning with this hearty egg and potato dish. It's great for serving the brunch crowd or overnight guests.

1 package (28 ounces)
   frozen potatoes O'Brien
2 teaspoons seasoned salt
½ teaspoon ground black
   pepper
1 package (8 ounces)
   shredded 2% colby-jack
   cheese (divided)
8 eggs
2 cups milk
¼ cup flour

Arrange potatoes in 9x13-inch baking dish that has been coated with no-stick cooking spray. Season with seasoned salt and pepper. Top with 1 cup of the cheese. In medium bowl, beat together eggs and milk. Whisk in flour. Pour mixture over potatoes. Cover and refrigerate overnight.

Uncover and bake in 350° F oven for 30 minutes. Top with remaining cheese. Bake until golden brown and set, about 10 minutes. Let stand 5 minutes before serving.

Makes 8 servings

Per serving

Calories 305
Fat 16 g
Cholesterol 242 mg
Sodium 700 mg
Carbohydrate 24 g
Fiber 2 g

Bistro French Toast

What could be an easier brunch accompaniment than French toast from the oven? Topped with preserves and dusted with powdered sugar, c'est magnifique!

3 eggs, slightly beaten
1 cup milk
¼ cup almond-flavored
   liqueur (Amaretto), OR
   1 teaspoon almond
   extract plus enough milk
   to equal ¼ cup
2 teaspoons vanilla extract
¼ teaspoon ground
   nutmeg
1 loaf (8 ounces) French
   baguette, cut into
   1-inch slices
½ cup black cherry, apricot
   or other preserves, melted
Powdered sugar
Maple syrup (optional)

In medium bowl, combine eggs, milk, liqueur, vanilla and nutmeg. Coat 9x13-inch baking dish with no-stick cooking spray. Lightly spread melted preserves over bread. Arrange in baking dish, preserves-side up. Pour egg mixture evenly over bread. Let stand until egg is absorbed, about 5 to 10 minutes.

Bake in 425° F oven until lightly browned, about 12 to 15 minutes. Sprinkle powdered sugar over toast before serving. If desired, serve with maple syrup.

Makes 8 servings

Per serving

Calories 202
Fat 3 g
Cholesterol 82 mg
Sodium 212 mg
Carbohydrate 35 g
Fiber 1 g

recipes

Brandy Sauce

Per 2 tablespoons

Calories 52
Fat 3 g
Cholesterol 8 mg
Sodium 185 mg
Carbohydrate 1 g
Fiber 1 g

2 tablespoons butter
  (divided)
1 medium onion, chopped
1 carrot, chopped
1 rib celery, chopped
2 large cloves garlic, minced
¼ cup brandy
1 can (14 ounces) beef broth
1 tablespoon cornstarch,
  dissolved in 1 tablespoon
  water
Drippings from roasting pan
  (optional)
Salt and freshly ground
  black pepper to taste

In medium skillet, melt 1 tablespoon of the butter over medium-high heat. Add onion, carrot, celery and garlic; cook stirring occasionally until vegetables are browned, about 5 minutes. Stir in brandy; cook until liquid evaporates, about 1 minute. Add broth and bring to a boil. Reduce heat and simmer for 5 minutes.

Strain vegetables from broth and discard. Return sauce to skillet; bring to a boil. Stir in cornstarch mixture and cook until thickened, about 1 minute. If desired, deglaze roasting pan with 2 tablespoons water, stirring to scrape browned bits from bottom of pan; stir into sauce.

Remove sauce from heat and whisk in remaining 1 tablespoon butter. Season with salt and pepper.

Makes 1 cup

Mudega Sauce

Per 2 tablespoons

Calories 51
Fat 3 g
Cholesterol 9 mg
Sodium 182 mg
Carbohydrate 2 g
Fiber <1 g

2 tablespoons butter
1 package (3 ounces) sliced
  prosciutto, cut into strips
½ cup sliced mushrooms
½ cup finely chopped onion
2 cloves garlic, minced
1 cup low-sodium chicken or
  beef broth
1 cup Madeira wine
1 tablespoon fresh lemon
  juice
1 tablespoon cornstarch
3 tablespoons water
¼ cup half-and-half

In large skillet, melt butter over medium heat. Add prosciutto, mushrooms, onion and garlic; cook stirring constantly until onion is tender, about 4 to 5 minutes. Add broth, wine and lemon juice; bring to a boil. Reduce heat and simmer until heated through.

In 1-cup glass measure, dissolve cornstarch in water; stir in half-and-half. Slowly stir into sauce; simmer until slightly thickened, about 2 to 3 minutes.

Makes 2 cups

Jack Daniel's Sauce

1 tablespoon olive oil
1 small white onion,
   coarsely chopped
2 ribs celery, coarsely
   chopped
1 carrot, coarsely chopped
1 cup Jack Daniel's whiskey
2 cans (10.5 ounces each)
   double-strength beef
   broth
1 tablespoon tomato paste
2 bay leaves
6 whole black peppercorns
2 sprigs fresh rosemary
2 tablespoons butter,
   softened
2 tablespoons flour

In large skillet, heat olive oil over medium-high heat. Add vegetables; cook stirring frequently until vegetables are brown, about 8 to 10 minutes. Remove from heat; cool for 5 minutes (to prevent flaming of whiskey).

Add whiskey; stir to scrape browned bits from bottom of pan. Place pan over medium heat; simmer until sauce reduces to 1/2 cup, about 5 minutes. Add broth, tomato paste, bay leaves, peppercorns and rosemary; bring to a boil. Reduce heat and simmer until sauce reduces to 1 1/2 cups, about 8 to 10 minutes.

Strain vegetables and herbs from sauce and discard. Return sauce to skillet. In small bowl, stir together butter and flour. Whisk into sauce. Cook stirring constantly until sauce has thickened slightly, about 1 to 2 minutes.

Makes 1 1/2 cups

Per 2 tablespoons

Calories 96
Fat 4 g
Cholesterol 6 mg
Sodium 402 mg
Carbohydrate 3 g
Fiber 1 g

Marsala Sauce

1 tablespoon butter
1/2 cup sliced cremini
   mushrooms
1 tablespoon flour
3/4 cup chicken, beef or
   vegetable broth
1/2 cup dry Marsala wine
Salt and pepper to taste

In medium skillet, melt butter over medium heat. Add mushrooms; cook until lightly browned. Stir in flour; cook 1 to 2 minutes. Add broth and wine; cook stirring constantly until slightly thickened, about 3 minutes. Season with salt and pepper.

Makes 1 cup

TIP Choose chicken, beef or vegetable broth to complement the entrée with which the sauce will be served.

Per 2 tablespoons

Calories 37
Fat 2 g
Cholesterol 4 mg
Sodium 102 mg
Carbohydrate 2 g
Fiber <1 g

No-Fail Hollandaise Sauce

Per 2 tablespoons

Calories 91
Fat 10 g
Cholesterol 75 mg
Sodium 106 mg
Carbohydrate 1 g
Fiber 0 g

1/2 cup butter
3 egg yolks, lightly beaten
2 tablespoons heavy
  whipping cream,
  at room temperature
2 tablespoons fresh lemon
  juice
1/2 teaspoon dry mustard
1/4 teaspoon salt

Place butter in 2-cup glass measure. Microwave (high) for 1 minute or until butter is melted; set aside. In small bowl, combine egg yolks, cream, lemon juice, dry mustard and salt. Whisk until smooth. Slowly whisk egg mixture into melted butter. Microwave (medium-50% power) for 1 minute, whisking every 20 seconds, until sauce is thick and smooth.

Makes 1 1/2 cups

TIP Sauce can be made ahead, covered and refrigerated overnight. To warm, microwave on medium-50% power for 1 to 2 minutes, whisking every 30 seconds until smooth.

Béarnaise Sauce

Per 2 tablespoons

Calories 143
Fat 16 g
Cholesterol 92 mg
Sodium 159 mg
Carbohydrate 1 g
Fiber 0 g

1/2 cup butter
1/4 cup heavy whipping
  cream, at room
  temperature
2 egg yolks, beaten
1 tablespoon tarragon
  vinegar or white wine
  vinegar
1 tablespoon finely
  chopped onion
1/2 teaspoon dry mustard
1/2 teaspoon dried tarragon
1/4 teaspoon salt

Place butter in 2-cup glass measure. Microwave (high) for 1 minute or until butter is melted. Whisk in remaining ingredients. Microwave (medium-50% power) for 3 minutes, whisking every minute, or until thickened.

Makes 1 cup

Equivalents

Pinch or dash	= less than 1/8 teaspoon
1 tablespoon	= 3 teaspoons
1 fluid ounce	= 2 tablespoons
1/4 cup	= 4 tablespoons
1/3 cup	= 5 tablespoons + 1 teaspoon
1 cup	= 16 tablespoons or 8 fluid ounces
1 cup	= 1/2 pint
1 pint	= 2 cups or 16 fluid ounces
1 quart	= 2 pints or 32 fluid ounces
1 gallon	= 4 quarts
1 pound	= 16 ounces
2 slices bread	= 1 cup soft bread crumbs
1 medium lemon	= 3 tablespoons juice, 2 to 3 teaspoons zest
1 medium lime	= 1 1/2 to 2 tablespoons juice, 1 teaspoon zest
1 medium orange	= 1/3 to 1/2 cup juice, 1 1/2 to 2 tablespoons zest
1 stick butter	= 1/2 cup, 1/4 pound, or 8 tablespoons
1 cup uncooked rice	= 3 cups cooked rice
1 rotisserie chicken (3 pounds)	= 3 cups shredded cooked chicken
3/4 pound boneless, skinless chicken breast	= about 2 cups diced cooked chicken
1 bottle (750 ml) wine	= about 3 1/4 cups (25.4 fluid ounces)
4 ounces cheese	= 1 cup crumbled, grated or shredded

How Much Meat Should I Buy?

As you plan your menu, you want enough to serve everyone comfortably without necessarily having leftovers for days on end. Here's a little help with your shopping list.

In general, plan on 3 to 4 servings per pound of boneless meats, like chicken breasts, ground meats, fish, pork chops, steaks and roasts.

Bone-in cuts are a little more challenging. Allow for the weight of the bone when determining how much to purchase.

Bone-In	Servings Per Pound
Beef	
Short Ribs	1 to 2
Standing Rib Roast	1 to 2
Steak	2 to 3
Pork	
Chops	2 to 3
Roast	2 to 3
Ham	2 to 3
Poultry	
Cornish Hens	1 to 2
Chicken, whole	2
Turkey Breast	2
Turkey, whole	1
Fish	
Shrimp, in shell	3 to 4

Is It Done?

When it comes to determining the doneness of meat, fish and poultry, looks alone can be deceiving. Here are some helpful hints for delicious results every time.

Thermometers

Using a thermometer is the most accurate way to determine whether food is done. Insert the thermometer into the center of the meat. Avoid touching fat, bone or stuffing. See page 14 for how to check the temperature of thin cuts of meat.

Meat thermometers have large dials that indicate the temperature and sometimes have a scale that describes the doneness (rare, medium, well). They are oven-safe and designed to be inserted in the food at the beginning of the cooking time and left in while it cooks.

Instant-read thermometers take a food's temperature in seconds. They have smaller dials and are inserted in food near the end of cooking time just long enough to check the temperature. These thermometers are not oven-safe.

Minimum Safe Internal Temperatures
(The internal temperature will rise 5 to 10 degrees during standing time.)

Ground beef and pork	155° F
Beef, rib roast	130° F (*medium*)
Beef, steak	·
Rare	140° F (*not recommended*)
Medium	145° F
Well	170° F (*not recommended*)
Fish	145° F
Pork, chops, roast, tenderloin	145 to 150° F
Pork, sausage	155° F
Chicken, boneless skinless breast	165° F
Chicken, whole	170° F
Chicken, dark meat	170° F
Cornish hen	165° F
Turkey breast	165° F

Stop! Put down that knife and let the meat rest before carving or slicing. Juices rise to the surface during cooking and need a few minutes to settle back into the meat. Tent the meat loosely with foil – don't wrap tightly – and let the meat rest. About 5 to 10 minutes is perfect for steaks; about 10 minutes for pork tenderloin; and about 15 to 20 minutes for large roasts, whole chickens or turkeys. Proper standing time makes meats easier to carve into neat slices, and each bite will be tender and juicy.

Dierbergs School of Cooking

Dierbergs School of Cooking Locations

Southroads Center
Tesson Ferry and I-270
St. Louis, MO 63128

West Oak Center
Olive Boulevard and
    Craig Road
Creve Coeur, MO 63141

Clarkson/Clayton Center
Clarkson and Clayton Roads
Ellisville, MO 63011

Bogey Hills Plaza
Zumbehl Road and I-70
St. Charles, MO 63303

Edwardsville Crossing
Troy Road and
    Governor's Parkway
Edwardsville, IL 62025

636-812-1336 (Missouri)
618-622-5353 (Illinois)

For more information on Dierbergs publications,
Dierbergs School of Cooking or cooking class schedules:
www.dierbergs.com

Index

◆ Photograph of Recipe
♥ Heart Healthy Recipe
Items in italic are sidebars